# THE ARCHIE MOORE STORY

# THE ARCHIE MOORE STORY
# BY ARCHIE MOORE

**Originally published in 1960**

*This book is for my wife, Joan,*
*and for my two daughters, Rena and Joan*

*I would like to thank my good friend
Bob Condon for helping me to find the
best way to tell the story of my life.*

*I would also like to thank Dave Gregg,
who encouraged me to do this book.*

# CONTENTS

# ROUND 1 THE EARLY DAYS

They say Methuselah lived 900 years, and I've never heard anyone accuse him of lying about his age. By the beard of the Prophet I'm just a kid, yet everyone seems to want to age me faster than bathtub gin. Some relatives and many sports writers have pegged my age from forty-two to fifty. Some even claim I was too old for World War I. My age, like reports of Mark Twain's death, has been greatly exaggerated.

Take my word for it. I was born in Benoit, Mississippi, on December 13, 1916. I'm proud of my age and the fact that I've beaten fighters who were young enough to be my sons. I'm fast approaching middle age, and as of this writing I'm Light Heavyweight Champion of the World and if I should happen to be fifty and hold that title I've certainly put some pep into a lot of guys in that age bracket. Age is what you make it, and I've jabbed it far out in front of me. Right now I'm as happy as a pig in mud. I've got my wonderful family, my title, a beautiful home and possibly a new career as an actor stretching out before me. Kids can't appreciate that kind of contentment. I know; I was a kid once. . . .

I was born Archie Lee Wright. My mother Lorena was fifteen when my sister Rachel was born, and I came along two years later. Before I was out of infancy my parents separated and I was given into the tender care of my uncle and aunt, Mr. and Mrs. Cleveland

Moore. I became Archie Lee Moore, for it saved many questions put to my aunt when we moved from house to house throughout the years. Moore is my name, and it is the name my children have. I have never felt any resentment toward my mother, as circumstances forced her to do just what she did. For without my uncle and aunt I would be Archie Lee "Nothing."

We read so much today about high-school students becoming engaged and even married while still in their teens. It may work for a few, but the responsibilities of marriage are far more serious than the romantic ideas conjured up beneath a glowing moon during an intermission at a school prom. My parents married young and regretted it. I married young and it failed. Survival, in itself, is tough enough, but to fend for a wife and two children proved to be too much for my father, and so my aunt Willie Pearl Moore stepped in and took over the care and welfare of Rachel and Archie. My physical inheritance came from a combination of a small father, Thomas Wright, and his tall and slender wife.

My uncle and aunt lived in St. Louis and it was there I lived through most of my childhood. I still think of St. Louis as my home, although San Diego adopted me early in my career and I now live comfortably in a dream house I have been building in my mind during more than twenty-five years of fighting. My aunt lives in the house adjoining mine and is now helping my wife Joan raise my two daughters, Rena and Joan. Knowing my auntie I can see the day when my grandchildren will race across the lawn to see what Auntie has in the refrigerator. She is a woman without children of her own, yet a mother in the finest and noblest sense of the word.

The move of the Negro from South to North in those days forty years ago was an economic migration. My Uncle Cleveland was a laborer. He was a hard-working, dependable man who was employed every week of the year at all kinds of manual labor. His reputation for reliability kept him in constant demand. We ate well and lived well as a result of his industry. Uncle Cleveland worked hard during the week and only took one day for diversion. He would have his "pint" Saturday night and play cards, and after relaxing on Sunday he would be back at work Monday to support his new-found family. He was a fine man—to me the finest man I ever met—and on his deathbed he made me promise to take care of my sister and my auntie. This was an occasion that made a deep impression upon me, and today I can say I kept my promise as best I knew how.

He was an inspiration to me in more ways than one. He was a beautifully developed physical specimen, having 17-inch biceps and about an 18-inch neck, with sloping shoulders and a huge, deep chest. I can easily recall watching him as he washed his face in the washbasin we had, watching his muscles quiver and ripple as I wished silently to have muscles such as those. In later years I used to walk on my hands and chin the bar 255 times to attain the powerful arms my uncle once had. When I buy clothing now I think I overdid it.

They say you never miss the water until the well runs dry, and more and more I miss my Uncle Cleveland. I'm certain the women in my family appreciate my accomplishments, but just think of the thrill it would have been to have had my Uncle Cleveland seated ringside when I defeated Joey Maxim for the world title!

After starting school in St. Louis, it was my auntie's custom to have my sister and me spend our vacations with our grandparents in Mississippi. There were cousins our own age, and the vacation was something to anticipate. They lived, of course, in a house just a little better than a shack but my grandfather farmed his own land. He was not a sharecropper, and in Mississippi in those days it made a big difference in his social standing in his own community. There were four rooms in the shack which stood on my grandfather's forty or fifty acres. An outhouse was in the back and we slept on straw beds. But outside was nature. In the summer the fish were jumpin' and the sweet, fresh smell of melons on the vine was in the air. All around us were watermelon and cantaloupe, with the cotton in blossom in the fields beyond making the farmhouse seem like an oasis in the Arctic. We had chickens, corn and white fresh butter. When company came a hog was killed, and often Grandfather would send juicy hams to

St. Louis and my auntie would wonder who had visited them. We used to pick a nice fat melon—Georgia ham as we called them—and lower it in the bucket of the well. By nightfall it was cold and delicious, and we kids, like all kids, would spit the pits at one another by snapping them through our teeth. There was a swimming hole and long hours spent wading in the creek. It was a joyous time for the city cousins, and my sister and I used to look forward to summer with an anticipation of taste pleasures and fun that has never had its equal to this day.

As a very small child I had never been told of the social differences between the black and white races. I suppose the Negro, from the time he was shipped to this country in the dank and foul holds of slave ships, has had instilled in him *fear*. It is a word shunned by everyone and I believe the hope of the modern black man is to face this complicated feeling and work towards social recognition based on achievement and advancement accomplished by the Negro race for itself and for the community in which he lives.

But being in the age of innocence I never felt this fear, for my aunt was more concerned in teaching me right from wrong, as she knew there would come a time when I would have to make my own decisions, and the values I believed in would make me act correctly nine times out of ten. But that tenth time is often just enough to teach a young Negro that sometimes black is wrong but white is always right. One such summer vacation brought the color difference into startling clarity of focus for me. Up until that day, and I was eight years old, I had never experienced nor knew about racial prejudices.

One warm summer's morning my sister, my cousin and I were riding an old swaybacked horse of my grandfather's. We, being city kids, were perched precariously in the middle of the sway, holding the horse's mane in a deathlike clutch, while our cousin led the placid beast down the road. The fast pace of about a mile an hour was too much for my sister, and she slid off to help my cousin control this fugitive from a rodeo. Suddenly, from the bushes alongside the road, a small white boy leaped out to confront our caravan. He knew my cousin and they exchanged greetings. Without warning the boy broke a switch off a bush and swung it violently at the horse, which caused him to rear up and throw me off his back. My reflexes saved me from being trampled, and almost in the same motion as I scrambled out of the way of those big hoofs, I grabbed the boy by his shirt front and shook him in rage. I kept shouting, asking why he had done a thing like that. Had he been trying to make the horse hurt me? Little did I know that the apprehension on his face wasn't caused by my yelling and shaking him but came as a result of his surprise of a sheltered white Mississippian being abused by a colored boy. He began to cloud up but didn't cry and then broke loose and ran off.

The horse and I were now alone. I took a quick count and saw my cousin running helter-skelter down the road clutching my sister's hand and dragging her behind him. I guess he intended to salvage what he could of the Moore family. I was too small to get back upon the horse, so I took the halter and led him back down the hot, dusty road. The horse was the only one who dismissed the incident. When I arrived there was a great commotion and my auntie took me inside and implored me never to hit a white person. I replied I hadn't hit him and explained I might have fallen under the animal or perhaps my sister might have been trampled. Auntie didn't care about that, seeing we were both unharmed. She was emphatic. She wanted me to promise. I wouldn't; I couldn't. She grew angry because I wasn't submissive.

I am not submissive today. Nor am I aggressive in that sense of the word. I have no chip on my shoulder. But on that day it was made clear to me there was a difference in human beings based on the color of their skin. (Religious intolerance was a later revelation.) Here was the fear: the idea that one race is permitted to treat another badly for their own satisfaction. It has to be taught, however, for it was not born in me that there was any difference. When I grabbed that boy and shook him it wasn't because I was being devilish or mean. I thought I was right and, by the same token, I'm equally sure the other boy had no idea of plaguing me because I was a colored boy. It was a simple act of mischief on his part, that of a normal boy. As proof, nothing more came of his end of the incident and so I'm sure it was my anger and not my color that made him run off.

My aunt then said we would have to leave. Regardless of whether I promised or not, we would have to leave. When I asked why, I was told it was because I had hit a white boy and it would only cause trouble for the relatives who lived there if I stayed. Young as I was, I said that if I had to leave Mississippi for such a reason I would never return. I was then eight years old and I have never been back. Perhaps I'm too harsh, perhaps Mississippi misses me.

One other memory of Mississippi stands out in my mind. I was to think of it in later years when dieting became such an integral part of my life. There was an enormous woman living in Benoit who used to waddle past our front gate. Many kids used to walk behind her and mimic in her rolling wake as she sailed down the road. Being young we couldn't see the tragedy in being so heavy. One day my auntie and I were seated on the porch as she struggled by and I noticed a look of sympathy on my auntie's face. She looked at me and said, "Archie Lee, poor Mrs. Brown is heading straight for the cemetery."

The implication of death gave Mrs. Brown an aura of glamour to me. As kids we tried to understand death, but couldn't. But we knew it had some sort of finality and importance to adults. It was not of our world. I wondered just how Mrs. Brown could invite Mr. Death to come calling as I would have liked the information just for the having. I asked my aunt why Mrs. Brown was going to die.

"Archie Lee," she began, "there once was a farmer who irrigated his land with a little pump. And he was doing pretty good, so he bought a couple of more acres and he still did very well. He kept on and kept on and soon he had twice as much land as he started with."

"Why, Auntie," I said, "wasn't that smart to add more land?"

"Sure, addin' to the land was good, but that farmer made a fatal mistake. While he kept addin' to his property he didn't stop to figure the same little pump was doing more and more work, and it finally broke down."

Trying to hook Mrs. Brown and an irrigation pump was a little puzzling to me. I sat quietly while Auntie thought I was thinking, and at last she said, "Archie Lee, everybody is like a farm and we each have a heart that pumps for us. Some folks, for a good many reasons, take on more size than the good Lord intended and their hearts tire and break down, and when that happens they get their mail from the groundhog."

A few years later the great fighter Joe Gans was my hero. He was from Baltimore, and became Lightweight Champion of the World. I was a pest about Gans. I could listen to grown-ups talk about him for hours and read everything I could get my hands on that mentioned him. Then I read of his fight with Battling Nelson. Sportswriters said Gans was the better man, but Gans had to make 133 pounds ringside for his fight. Reducing drastically weakened him, and although he made the weight he lost the fight. He developed tuberculosis and died.

Old Mrs. Brown and Joe Gans called Mr. Death in different ways. She got heavier and heavier and taxed her heart and he foolishly abused his system with a weight reduction plan that weakened him beyond recall. My auntie's story about the little pump that failed and Gans' fight with Nelson stayed with me all my life, and helped me in later years when I devised my own plan for losing weight and retaining strength.

Those two incidents are the sharpest memories I have of my days in Mississippi. From then on St. Louis was the center of my universe and the big news of that childhood period was when my mother remarried. She became Mrs. Mordell Brown and my aunt and uncle wanted Rachel and me to know our mother, and so we visited the Browns on weekends. My mother and aunt are still very close and my mother frequently visits me in San Diego.

We lived "across the tracks" in a shotgun house. Three rooms straight through, with a toilet and a woodshed in the back yard. I have warm memories of those days. My sister and I, according to my aunt, were always helpful around the house. Even today, when I'm in training, I make my own bed when I get up in the morning, a habit carried over from my youth. I can remember having to stand on a chair to dry dishes as my sister washed them. Somehow I liked the responsibility, and maybe if all children had definite chores to do, day after day, there'd be less of this thing we call juvenile delinquency.

Mordell Brown, my mother's new husband, was a veteran of World War I, a former soldier whose army experiences fascinated me. He was a hard-working man like my uncle, and my sister and I liked him. When my father and mother separated I was only eighteen months old, and I cannot remember him from those days. Today my real father is in St. Louis in partnership with his brother, running a neighborhood grocery store.

Rachel and I acquired a half-brother, Samuel, who was promptly nicknamed Jackie. Unfortunately Mordell Brown died and my ever-ready aunt stepped in and Jackie became one of the family. We used to share the chores at home and one of our duties was to bring wood for the kitchen stove in from the shed in the backyard. I was mischievous and used to plague Sammy with stories of goblins and the like that lurked in the wood shed waiting for little boys to steal their wood. Other demons hid in his bedroom, and unless I was with him he was in for sore trouble. Of course Auntie heard nothing of this, as I had told Sammy about a very special demon who took care of little boys who "snitched" and who did so in broad daylight. That demon's name was Archie Lee. As of this writing Sammy is running a restaurant in San Diego and helps me train young fighters when his time allows.

Let me account for the rest of the family. My mother married once again and, in time, another half-brother, Louis, was on the scene. As Louis grew up it was apparent he was the sharpest of us all.

He had a quick and bright mind, and when I watch my oldest daughter Rena I'm reminded of brother Louis. He "caught on" to almost everything with the greatest of ease. But ease was his problem. If something couldn't be done the easy way it wasn't worth doing, according to Louis. He was a born gambler. He liked marbles, but when he discovered it took practice to develop the skill needed to win he shifted his view and took the easy way. He taught the other boys his age how to shoot craps, and soon Louis had a washtub full of marbles. He was a loan shark before he was in his teens and would lend five marbles and get back seven as interest on his loan. Louis pops up again in the story of my life, but much later on.

Dumas grade school was my first tilt with formal education. It was wisely situated next to the Loose-Wiles Biscuit Company, and for a nickel you could get a bag of broken cookies. A broken cookie is freshly baked and tastes just as good as a whole cookie, and a bagful looks like more than you can eat, although that never happened. The Dumas school had colored students only, but not due to any law, merely the fact that this was a colored neighborhood and that was the way the cookie crumbled. I was transferred from Dumas when we moved to another neighborhood. I suppose Uncle Cleveland had hit a tough period, as we moved to a railroad flat in a poorer section. I missed the Loose-Wiles Biscuit Company something fierce. But things got better and we moved to Biddle Street and I went to the Jefferson school. I liked school. I was fairly quick, and studying didn't bother me and I didn't bother studying. The teachers at Jefferson were both competent and patient. One teacher I remember was Miss Henderson, a prematurely gray-haired girl of about eighteen. I liked her then, and liked her when I met her recently and she looked just as pretty as she did when I stared at her from a school desk.

The first fight I ever recall having was with a boy named Johnny Cunningham. I knocked his tooth out. Today he is an undertaker, and as the old joke goes, I hope he will not box me again.

Mose Howell was my closest friend, one of a family of five brothers. One day, walking home from school, my sister Rachel was teasing Mose's brother Reuben. She egged him on and he finally slapped her. Reuben was four years older than I was, but my rage didn't take that into consideration. We fought, and my anger forced me to fight over my head and I held him even. It was my first draw. I was very proud that day of having defended Rachel and held my own with a boy bigger and heavier. But Mose took the incident coldly and sided with his brother. He finally sicced his dog Spot on me and I lost the seat of my pants. Dogs today can't aim the way they used to.

Every boy, at one time or another, dreams of running away from home, and surely many of them do. The romantic misery of picturing all the people you love suffering your loss as you trudge down the railroad tracks is an idea shared by all boys. I ran away from home once and I set the incident down as my claim to a normal childhood. I had become enraged at what I thought was an unfair decision. Sammy was kept after school and I was told to bring in wood in his place. We used to alternate at the chore and I resented getting the job two days in a row. Of such things are rebellions made. I took a few belongings and went through the backyard determined to make them rue the day they made Archie Lee do more than his share of work. I crossed the street and went into the back of a used car lot and found an old sedan. I curled up on the back seat and nibbled on the parcel of food I had stolen for my trip. I lay there wallowing in my misery and could hardly wait until the news got around that Archie Lee had run away from home. Along about nine-thirty the back seat got more and more uncomfortable. It was getting a bit cold, too. Now I began to think about the activities inside the house, with Rachel and Sammy doing their homework and Auntie sewing and Uncle Cleveland reading the paper. The radio would be on and maybe a good dance band would be playing softly in the background. Slowly I crawled out of the car and scuffed the dirt with my toe as I went back to the house. At the door I paused as I opened it and shouted to an imaginary friend, "G'night, y'all—see you tomorrow!" I entered, and my auntie stood waiting.

"Archie Lee, go into your room. I saw you leave and I saw you crawl into that old car. You can run away if you like but the next time bake your own biscuits. You took the ones I baked for supper, and that's what this spankin' is for. Stealin', not runnin' away." And that was the end of my Huckleberry Finn spirit.

I advanced in school and was now in the Lincoln School. It covered junior-high and high-school classes. It was a Negro high school. Lincoln was a fine school and it had been built in 1927 and it was shiny and clean. I then weighed 110 pounds and was too small for football. But my diet at home was excellent and I was quite strong for my weight. I liked to box and in my neighborhood was a fighter named Robert Johnson who used the ring name of Kid Roberts. He had a brother named Bat Grant and he taught him the rudiments of boxing. Bat, needing an opponent, taught me in turn, and Kid Roberts enjoyed watching us spar and would coach us as we went along. The Kid thought I had a flair for boxing and encouraged me—so much so that I got in quite a few fist fights and lost some and won some. At that time I was a regular attendant at church every Sunday and went to the Baptist Sunday school. My aunt had more to do with this habit than Kid Roberts.

Someone once asked me if I had been a juvenile delinquent. I admitted I had been. They asked me how I was able to change and I said, "I grew up." Sure, we had gangs in those days. Neighborhoods were composed of various groups of nationalities and races. The Italians, Jews, Irish and the Negroes all had gangs. We fought with fists and rocks. I saw very little "cutting" and almost never saw a gun. I do remember an incident when a friend of mine was beaten in a badly overmatched fight. The boy who beat him came back looking for him and my friend shot him. To this day I believe he was justified as he acted in self-defense. But ordinarily our gang fights were a far cry from the "rumbles" kids have today. We had no leather jackets with strange names written on the back. One gang was the Irish from Kerry Patch and the other was the gang from Jewtown.

Today's newspapers have glamorized street gangs, and each tries to outdo the other. Kids have very little balance of values, and when grown-ups make a big hullabaloo over violence they attempt greater violence to gain the attention they desire. In my day a passing grown-up could rout a gang fight just with his adult authority. Nowadays kids attack cops with no fear of law at all. I never failed to get a whipping from my aunt if I came home with a black eye or a bloody nose. She would allow me to fight under supervision in a gymnasium or in a friend's cellar, but street fighting was *verboten*. Parents of gang kids today are asking for revenge if they lay a hand on the junior Dillinger. Our gangs usually fought over fancied slights or invasion of enemy territory. But most often the two gangs would meet and a representative of one fought a fair fight with a representative "champion" of the enemy. When it was over the two fighters shook hands and peace was temporarily restored between the warring tribes. It was actually fair play in practice, and this settlement of differences with a possible black eye or a bloody nose was far better than a serious knife wound or a fatal bullet from a zip gun.

My sister and I had always been very close. Not in our daily activities, naturally, as she had her friends and I had mine. But in the evenings we always had time to talk together and we walked to school together (Sammy, being younger, didn't attend the same school), but now I noticed we were slowly drifting apart. She was two years older than I and, being a woman, matured more quickly. She was beginning to like a boy, Elihu Williams, and that was an interest I couldn't share with her; she had no inclination to talk to me about this and I certainly had no inclination to listen. I had two pals, Robert Stamps and Pretty Eddie Williams, and we had a common bond in prizefighting. They both could have become good fighters if they had had the proper coaching. But none of us knew at the time that I was destined to be a professional fighter. I wish they had known it then and showed a little more respect when we sparred.

Rachel's interest in Elihu became serious and they were married. He was the only man in her life. She rented an apartment in a nice neighborhood and it was my great pleasure to visit my married sister every other day or so and have a dish of peaches or a slice of her homemade cake. I'd sit with Rachel and we'd talk by the hour. We talked of Auntie and Uncle Cleveland. I dreamed of the day when I'd be an uncle myself, as I thought uncles were the greatest people on earth. But Rachel died in childbirth. It was a terrible loss to all of us. I loved my sister more than I can say. Even now, after all these years, I cannot bear to think of her as dead. Rachel gave birth to twins. The baby boy lived for four months and then joined his mother. The girl, of course, was immediately given to Auntie and now lives with her next door to me in San Diego. Her name is June and she and Auntie are as devoted as ever.

My Uncle Cleveland didn't live long enough to know his beloved Rachel had died. He passed away before the twins were born. It was a senseless and needless tragedy. He was being initiated into a fraternal organization and part of the initiation was physical punishment. An accident occurred which resulted in paralysis and eventual death. I would rather not name the organization, as no one was held accountable and the lamentable system of accepting new members has been drastically changed. This happened during the days of the deep depression. I clearly remember my uncle lying helpless on his bed. He called me in the day he died and made me promise to take care of Auntie for as long as she lived. Here he was, a man who willingly took in and supported four children literally by the sweat of his brow. Never a complaint, with only a few drinks on Saturday night to lighten his burden. And he was lying before me asking me to take care of my auntie. I made the promise gladly, and except for an occasional slip or two I believe kept the faith he had in me.

His death left my aunt with some money. He had insurance for $3,500, and for people in our circumstances that was very good. Also, two lodges paid death benefits of about $400 each. But my aunt was inexperienced in handling money, and kinfolk who knew her soft heart leeched on her and she would keep taking money out of the bank when none was going in. We were soon on welfare along with most of our neighbors, getting tinned beef (from Argentina), a sack of potatoes and a bi-monthly check. These were hard days for all of us, but most of all for my too-generous aunt.

After my uncle's death I began to run wild, not from feelings of insecurity but for personal monetary reasons. I thought I could become a great musician and I wanted a trumpet. Fighting was always with me but I had never considered becoming a professional, for I was much too young. But music really knows no age and I felt I could embark on that career immediately. My aunt, in better days, had gotten a piano, but I only desired a trumpet or a saxophone. Somewhere my aunt had read the obituary of an old steamboat musician, Charley Creath. The obituary writer had colorfully written that Charley had blown his lungs out, and my aunt believed this as true gospel. She flatly refused to help me get a trumpet. I began to indulge in petty thievery, thinking to save enough money to buy a horn. But I never saved a penny. I had a kindly schoolteacher, Miss Ellis, who was quite fond of me, and since I knew my aunt would never aid in my desire I asked Miss Ellis for help. But somehow when I spoke to her I asked for a pair of boxing gloves instead. I put no mystic interpretation on this switch of purpose; it was merely that she knew of my boxing, whereas a nebulous career as a musician might have seemed absurd to her, and so it came out—boxing gloves. Naturally these would cost far less than a trumpet, and perhaps I was entertaining thoughts of promoting Miss Ellis if she said yes and would go on from gloves to shoes and finally the coveted trumpet. Miss Ellis suggested I shop the hock shops and find a pair at a good price and, at the same time, she asked me to keep an eye out for a good oil lamp, which she needed. I knew we had two oil lamps at home and I stole them and sold them to Miss Ellis for a dollar apiece, and that's how I got the money for the first pair of boxing gloves I ever owned.

I should have worn the boxing gloves the clock around. But I became adept at light-fingered lifting along with the rest of my gang.

We started stripping empty houses, taking the lead pipes out and selling them, and cutting the wiring for the copper in it. There was nothing sinister about this. It was survival on our own terms. Like hunting for the pot or hunting for sport. We were not a bunch of junior Raffles pitting wits against the law. But, let's face it, we stole. I had a pal named Arthur James. His nickname was Knox. The hat company put out a cap that was very popular in those days and Knox wore his constantly. His mother was very kind to me and later proved to be a true Good Samaritan. Knox and I met in school and when I left school and turned myself loose on the streets he was always there.

It was inevitable that I would be caught. I think I knew this even before I started, but somehow the urge to have a few cents in my pocket made me overlook this eventuality. So I was caught. I was caught three times. The third time I had stolen money from a streetcar. Arthur would pull down the pole that carried the current from the overhead wire and when the motorman went back to investigate I would leap aboard like Jesses James and get the petty change from the motorman's box. The division of labor on a caper such as this was not arrived at by reasoning, and so it happened that mine was the more dangerous job, inasmuch as an off-duty cop helped me off with the box on my last "job." I was sentenced to three years in the reform school and eventually served twenty-two months.

While I was in the House of Detention awaiting sentence, another boy and I had a fight. Not a grudge fight, but there didn't seem to be anything else to do. He was tough. So tough I broke my left hand on him.

The reform school, now known as the Missouri Training School, was located at Booneville, and I was assigned to the brickyard. The brickyard was considered tough duty, and was purposely used to instill discipline in new "students." But my injured hand made it impossible to handle bricks and I was transferred to the laundry, where the work was lighter but the scalding steam and summer weather made the laundry hotter than jailhouse coffee. During my thinking hours, and I had plenty of them, I decided to make fighting my career. The reform school was my personal crossroads. I had burned the bridge of formal education behind me and I now had a choice of which way to go and what to do. The feeling of shame that came over me when I thought of how my auntie must feel made the good she had built into me come forth. I knew I needed a shortcut if I was to accomplish anything. Baseball was out. A man who made three hundred a season in Negro ball was considered to be doing well. Satchel Paige was the only man who was making so-called big money. Kid Chocolate was my hero at that time. Fighters like the Kid and John Henry Lewis were drawing gates of four to six thousand and getting 20 percent for themselves. A good main-event fighter could get $750, and that decided me. The study of music was too long a road and too uncertain. I loved music, but if after years of study I didn't have it where would I be? I loved to box and so, after weighting all the factors, I determined to learn as much as I could, strengthen myself and turn professional as soon as I was of age.

I was fifteen going on sixteen at this time and I had only seen one professional fight. Benny Deathpane, a well-known fighter of the time, fought an outdoor bout and I had peeked through the fence and marveled at his skill. The crowd, the noise and the fierce action intrigued me. I was all too aware of the obvious. I had the skill, the desire, and I wanted the money. Fighting was the answer.

My uncle had persuaded me to join the junior Mason's Drill Team, so discipline in the reform school was no problem to me. Even now I can remember names from those days. Colonel Ziske was the superintendent, and there was Major White, Major Johnson and Captains Mitchell and Young. I also recall Reverend Mundell, a minister who visited occasionally, and one particular day when he was dining and I was waiting table. I served from the wrong side and the matron, Mrs. John Little, called out to correct me. I got flustered and spilled the whole tray of coffee over the Reverend. I truly expected an unexpurgated course in Latin, but he was most understanding and I have always remembered his kindness.

One of the reasons I was grateful was that punishment at the institution was quite severe. The two greatest crimes were attempted escape and any sex offense. Boys guilty of either were beaten with a leather belt a quarter-inch thick and 4 inches wide. The belt was attached to a wooden handle and the strokes were administered with hearty enthusiasm. I had seen boys beaten until their work pants were stuck to their buttocks with blood. I didn't know what the punishment would be for scalding a minister but I suppose this little reminder of the eternal heat of hell strengthened his own good works. I have never drunk coffee with a minister since that day, as I feel I would be pushing my luck.

I boxed in reform school. I boxed, not fought. We were permitted a certain amount of play time, and boxing was a great outlet for frustrated emotions. We were encouraged in this, and boxing actually aided me in behaving. I got a good reputation, inasmuch as I scored sixteen knockouts in my first year. Other boys, prone to arguing and picking fights, left me strictly alone. I never felt the leather belt.

There were nine groups of boys in the school, arranged in alphabetical companies. The colored boys were in Company C. We actually had two companies, Big C and Little C. This was a type of integrated reform school. It was separate, but equal. But there was no real color line in reform school. Troubles shared form a true democracy. We were all in the same boat, and the Noah in charge didn't care if you were green or red. I was only punished once and I was beaten with a switch. I can still remember that old switch whistling when it came around at me. But I got around it just as I get around an opponent in the ring. I crowded the switch. It lashed around my backside but the true force of the whipping fell upon my legs. Even when my auntie used to flail at me in exasperation I would crowd in close and her arms, lacking leverage, would inflict no hurt at all.

Arthur "Knox" James turned up at reform school. I had been expecting him. Somehow most of us in that finishing school felt all our friends would turn up sooner or later. And most times we were right. It was the place to go in our set.

I remember one fellow in "school" who taught me where Kid Roberts left off. His name was Eddie "Louisiana" Jones and he was three years older than I. He groomed me, and as I said I scored sixteen knockouts but finally was matched against Robert Woods, whose nickname was Al Jolson. He gave me my first defeat. He gave me more than that, but I have a gift for understatement when talking of my losses.

In the Little C company there was a boy named Jack Alexander who was the mascot of the whole school. He hadn't committed any crime but he was an orphan, and as there was no one to take care of him he was sent to the reform school. He had been there since he was a baby and would stay there until he was eighteen. Somehow the plight of this boy touched all the wild kids in the school. All of us, no matter how bad, had had some contact with love. Behind each boy there was a mother, sister, aunt or grandmother who had cared. I don't mention male relatives, because I have found boys respond in most part to the affection of female relatives. It may be that girls respond to male relations. I don't know. But many a night we would whisper to each other, and since the stirrings of sex were unknown we would talk of things we knew about. Home cooking, spankings and what the gang did. When I say sex was unknown I mean it in the sense that knowledge and practice are two different things. Certainly there was perversion in the school and you could participate or ignore it. I think moral character is a very pliable thing, and it bends to circumstance. I had no trouble avoiding the secret conclaves known to everyone in the school but I do not hold that I was morally above it. I wasn't interested and I wasn't tempted. But if society condones penning men up with no possible release, then society must condone the practices that result.

Much has been written about reform schools. Men far wiser than I have written volumes on the subject. My authority is attendance. I know that the Missouri Training School for Boys no longer uses the leather belt. And without psychological reasons I can state the school is better for abolishing this barbaric practice. I know, too, that recreational therapy is employed to channel energies and imaginations. The reform school world I lived in has vanished and I don't pine for the bad old days. I live to see the day when teenagers and even those younger are dealt with by entirely different methods, and I believe it will happen. To this day my recollections of reform school are always coupled with the idea I was punished for being caught. I never realized the fact that I was punished for stealing. Stealing was such an everyday way of life that it was accepted by all of us. But to the inmates of reform school, we were there because we had been caught. Nothing else.

The school was self-sustaining. It had, beside the brickyard and laundry, an orchard, a dairy, bake shop, stone quarry and butcher shop. They say our rehabilitation started the day the gate clanged shut on us, but no matter how well the rehabilitation went the stealing worsened. We stole from the shops, from each other and from the guards. I smoked merely because it wasn't permitted and because the challenge was so great. You could only get cigarettes by stealing them from one of the guards or officers, and if you were smoking the other boys knew how you had acquired the cigarette, and your respect for yourself was reflected in the attitude of the boys in your company.

It was time for my discharge, my parole. I hadn't served my full term but I had gotten an allowance for good behavior (I hadn't been caught) and was eligible to be paroled *if* I had a job to go to on the outside. My mother went to the parole officer, Sgt. Thomas Moran, and he found a sales position for me with an ice and coal dealer. I was released in his custody and he turned me over to a playground superintendent named Thomas Brooks (now a captain on the St. Louis police force, as is Moran). I learned that Brooks had actually gotten me this job. I fondly remember both these men. They treated me like a man. They didn't lecture, nor did they have to. I had had enough of prison, no matter if it was called a school. At least penal servitude does accomplish that much in many cases. Now, resolved to live better, I reported for work.

I had no coat. I was wearing clothes that were given me the day I left school, with the exception of my work brogans, which I had sold for two dollars. The shoes I wore had slits in the heel so I could get them on my ever-growin' feet. My boss was a little wizened Negro who explained that I was to stand on the step of the Model T pick-up truck he had and shout "Coal! Wood!" at the top of my lungs. We had a regular route, but this shouting was to attract extra customers. At each stop I would fill a bucket with coal; filled, the bucket weighed 80 pounds. I would carry this to the customer and return to my selling post on the back of the truck. My boss sat in the cab of the truck with a fur-trimmed coat turned up over his neck and a Russian fur hat pulled down over his ears. At his feet was another bucket filled with glowing coals. He was warm. There was very little reason for me to shout "Ice!" as the snow and slush was about 4 inches deep in the streets. The cold was unbearable, and I welcomed the opportunity of filling the bucket and carrying it flights of drafty stairs. It got me out of the biting wind. We made three trips to the coal yard that day, replenishing our wares, and finally, after twelve hours of bracing air the day's work was done. I had been promised a dollar a day and my auntie surely needed the money.

We returned to his office in the basement of a tenement and I hastened to the pot-bellied stove and rubbed my hands trying to restore the circulation. After a few moments of bliss I was aware the stove wasn't lit, for we had been out all day. No matter. I turned to the perspiring man who had hired me and asked if I was to get paid by the day or by the week. By the day, he replied, as he tossed me a half a dollar. He mumbled that business hadn't been too good that day. I wondered if he had lost his mind, because I was the one who carried the bucket and collected the money for each delivery.

His real reason was apparent. It was no secret that I had just been in reform school, and I probably wasn't the first kid this black Fagin had used. He felt sure I would take the money and shut up. He knew the terms of my parole called for a steady job. It is the only time in my life that I have felt capable of killing another man. There were two or three ice picks sticking in the wall, and I had an urge to grab two of them and stab him repeatedly with both hands. There I stood, hungry, tired, cold, and he sat before me warm, well-fed and rich. I held my temper in check only because I knew what would befall me if I so much as laid a hand on this miserable specimen. I threw the fifty cents at him and told him if he needed money that badly I didn't want it. My tail was truly between my legs as I slunk out, down the dark hallway to the steps that reached the street. As I went out I could hear him pleading with me to come back to work the next day. It strikes me that a lot of trouble in this world stems from cruelties done to people when they are impressionable and liable to think everybody will treat them in the same way. Luckily, my counselors, Moran and Brooks, sided with me and suggested I look for something to do on my own. Of course I reported to Mr. Brooks every day.

I told my auntie the whole story and I left nothing out. When I told her I had wanted to stab the cockroach who hired me my aunt nodded and told me she was proud. She agreed with me and said that holding my temper was the main thing I had gained from that day's experience—and it was worth much more than a dollar. But she tempered my almost martyrlike feeling by saying I had to get some kind of job as the grim alternative was a long fast before I was returned to the school. My heroic attitude was dampened, to say the least.

Just by chance I passed Knox's house. His mother was home and she asked me to sit down and have a piece of cake and a glass of milk. Mrs. James was affluent according to our community's standards. She worked at the St. Louis plant of the Liggett & Myers tobacco company where she sorted tobacco leaves. Knox's mother owned the fine home she lived in, and her fellow workers boarded with her. She charged $4.50 a week for room and board. That, plus her salary, made her the tycoon of hard times. I asked her if she could get me a job at the factory. She sadly shook her head. They were laying people off, just as every industry was, in those days. But she looked at me as a substitute for Arthur. I told her that Arthur and I were done with stealing and both of us were determined to do something worthwhile. It was no hardship for me to say that Arthur missed her. He did. We often talked about his mother and my auntie. Mrs. James suggested that I become her housekeeper. While she and the boarders were away at work I would wash the breakfast dishes, make beds, scrub floors and do anything that was required. After a brief discussion it was decided that I would work Wednesdays and Saturdays when she was off work and could supervise my chores. I accepted and was promised $3 every Saturday. Mrs. James earned $16 a week at the tobacco plant. Saturdays became sheer heaven, as Mrs. James set her best table on that day. I was always invited to dinner with the other boarders, and it represented two meals to me, because it meant Auntie didn't have to buy food for me on that day. Mrs. James was always making little purchases against the day Arthur would come home from reform school, and each time she did she would buy me a duplicate. I got shirts, socks, and underwear from Mrs. James. She not only loved me like a son; I was her son while Arthur was away. I repaid this kindness by doing extra chores when she was working. One day I scrubbed the front steps with lye and when she returned she thought they had been painted. I can remember my joy at her astonishment. With two days' work a week and some money coming in the pressure of parole eased considerably and things at home were better. I could now turn to fighting once again, although in actuality it would be the very first time I had done so sincerely. When Arthur finally returned, he and I would spar in the large front room of his house. My friend Arthur "Knox" James is now in Chicago. He is the engineer of a men's club downtown and is in charge of the steam room. Arthur is well respected and successful, but his main interest in life is cultivating roses. He has gotten quite a name in that field, and both of us feel that life has given each of us a reward far greater than we anticipated during our whispered conferences in the reform school dormitory in the long, long ago.

My boxing aspirations, unfortunately, were all my own. No one shared them. I was seventeen, muscled, not too heavy and totally without experience in the eyes of the men who made matches or managed fighters. I was just a pest. The Civilian Conservation Corps had just begun and the program was attracting many boys who couldn't find work and who were drains on the family's finances. It was outdoor work, supervised by the government, and it afforded Archie Lee Moore a chance to build muscles and send money home each month. I had to make up for that period in the reform school and this seemed to be ideal. I went to Sergeant Moran and told him what I wanted to do. It was necessary for him to have my parole lifted but he knew I had been working at Mrs. James' boardinghouse, and he recommended my joining the C.C.C.

I was enrolled as a member of Camp 3760 at Poplar Bluff, Missouri, and in a few days I said goodbye to Mrs. James and Arthur, to my auntie and the rest of my family and, without knowing it, to my childhood.

# ROUND 2 FIVE DOLLARS A MONTH

The Civilian Conservation Corps was an emergency measure designed to relieve the pressures placed on poverty-stricken depression families. It was a natural deterrent to juvenile delinquency. It got boys off the streets, got them food and shelter and permitted them to contribute to the support of their families. We earned $30 a month, and 25 of this was sent home. We were given $5 a month for high living.

The camp at Poplar Bluff, Missouri, was a brand-new one with fine pine floors which we kept in clean and shiny condition. Our army cots had not yet arrived and we slept wrapped in blankets on the floor. After my time at the reform school this way of life was like being a guest at a mountain resort.

We were in the Forestry Division, which cleared road sites for the engineers and surveyors. It was hard work but very toughening, just the kind of work I wanted to build my biceps and legs. I worked as though I was eventually going to own the road. The other boys thought I was a bit touched and constantly kidded me about the amount of work I did. I went relentlessly on, chopping, hacking and digging because I was in training for my biggest fight—the fight for the survival of the individual, Archie Moore.

It actually was a fight for life, for years later I had serious surgery performed and I believe that my conditioning at the C.C.C. camp spelled the difference between death and recovery.

We went to work in a one-ton stake-body truck. Our mattocks, shovels and axes were piled in with us and all the boys except me sat on the floor of the truck having a smoke or playing harmonicas. I stood behind the cab and would practice ducking, bobbing and weaving. When we drove through areas with primitive roads or no roads at all the branches of trees would lash back as the truck forced its way through. I would wait until the last split second before ducking away from these snapping arms. It was a dangerous game, but it gave me the boxing style I use today. In the prize ring an opponent has only two arms, and I've been pretty good at ducking and bobbing to avoid them. I've missed a few times but I reason that if I beat everyone I'd put myself out of business. Anybody who can reason that clearly can't be all bad.

Captain Parks was in charge of the Poplar Bluff camp and he was a very sports-minded man. I asked for his permission to organize a boxing team and he was enthusiastic in his encouragement. Extra-curricular activity was most important to boys in our age group, and sports of every variety were needed to tire the boys out even after a tough working day.

In addition to my contemplated boxing team the camp had an orchestra, a swimming team and a basketball unit. Captain Parks advised me to post a notice on the bulletin board asking for boys who were interested to contact me. Teaching others to box taught me. I developed my own skills by helping others. I beat everyone; that is, everyone who wanted to try, including the camp heavyweight, Bernard Carter. His nickname was Brute and he weighed 230 pounds, but he was a lazy fighter. He thought training was something old-timers needed. If I remember correctly, it was May of 1936 when the first Golden Gloves tournament (in the Missouri area) was held. Brute was the only member of the team who didn't compete. We had finals for the Poplar Bluff area and a boy named Galen Stone beat Carter. Brute had spent the night before the fight in town on a date with his girlfriend. Brute should be one of our leading bankers today, because having a steady girlfriend on $5 a month takes a genius at financial juggling.

All my other teammates won their bouts over the Southeastern and Missouri and Illinois boxers. I won and got to the finals and boxed in those against a boy named Courtland Shephard. Courtland fought under the name of Courtland Shultz. No doubt he wanted to box completely incognito. He beat me. Shephard-Shultz later became a popular West Coast fighter and then married a lovely actress. With the money he earned fighting he opened a restaurant and bar in Hollywood and raised fine children. Not in the bar but at home. I still see Sir Courtland Shephard-Shultz on my frequent trips to Los Angeles.

Around the C.C.C. camp, with everyone dressed alike, it was nice to have a separate identity. I never kidded myself that I was a big deal but I did have identity, and to a kid like me that was important. I won the tri-state sectional tournament and was a sort of celebrity in the camp. Our team showing was mighty impressive and Captain Parks was proud of what we had accomplished.

I remember a tournament fight I had with a boy named Bill Richardson. I knocked him down with a volley of head punches about one minute into round one. His brother was a professional fighter but, more important, he was the referee. He was furious at me and told me to keep my punches up. Since I had been hitting Bill in the head I would have missed him altogether if I threw my punches any higher. But the referee said I had fouled him and he gave his brother a rest to recover from the so-called foul. I got steamed at this and offered to fight him, too. I resolved not to hit Bill any place but his head, and if the referee wanted me to make chop meat of his brother's face that was all right with me. This kid needed his brother for a referee like a moose needs a hat rack. In the second round I dropped him with a left hook that spun his head like a top and he dropped to the canvas like four pounds of mashed potatoes. With his dear brother around, Bill didn't need any enemies. But I sure needed a few friends. As he grudgingly counted his brother out and raised my hand in victory, I heard a man at ringside say, "For two cents I'd shoot that nigger."

Captain Parks was at ringside and he heard the remark, too. He was wearing his army.45 and he climbed into the ring to escort me to my dressing room. He immediately ordered all the C.C.C. boys to get into the trucks and instructed the drivers to snap the seal on the governers so the trucks would be able to make time. The local people, never too friendly to us, were muttering and grumbling. The police chief advised me not to stop to change. They hustled me out to my truck and we took off. Captain Parks raced on ahead. Our trucks pulled into camp, and the entrance area had been lit with a big spotlight and Captain Parks stood there with a sub machine gun cradled in his arms. Very shortly a line of cars came roaring up loaded with the "townies," but the sight of the captain slowed them down a bit. He warned them the camp was government property and he would defend it as best he knew how. Like most mobs, this one, too, was cowardly. They grumbled a while longer and then got into their cars and returned to town. I was the big hero, but I frankly didn't feel too heroic.

Aside from work and boxing we were all fairly normal boys and we wanted to get home now and then to visit relatives and friends. But you can't hail a cab on $5 a month. A bunch of us decided to visit St. Louis by hopping a freight train. We were green at this and the train we caught was a local. We left at six-thirty in the evening and the train stopped at every dip in the road bed. I climbed on board a tank car. I think it carried molasses. I was standing and holding the rail that ran around the car and in my other hand I had my little bag with my fight equipment in it. Gloves, shoes, socks, trunks. I always hoped to pick up a club fight in town to make a few extra dollars. Suddenly I saw the boys in front of me run to the next car and climb the ladder. Instinct made me whirl around and I saw a man, florid-faced with rage, rushing at me with a club raised over his head. He swung and I weaved slightly. The club smashed on the steel side of the car. I slipped but fortunately fell straddling the catwalk. I remember my foot hit the spinning wheel. I dropped my bag and turned and ran after the other boys. I ran across the tops of six or seven boxcars before I met my friends. I never saw the brakeman again but without his club he would have been foolish to come after us. If he had hit me there could have been but one result—death. Why a man, during the depths of the depression, would try to murder a boy for the sake of a free ride on top of a boxcar is something I have never figured out. But as horrible and murderous as that brakeman was, some other kind Samaritan found my boxing bag and returned it to me intact. I have no idea who this was but I was grateful then, and I still am. Part of my gratitude was for the equipment but a bigger part was due to his restoring my faith in people after such a narrow and needless escape.

At seven-thirty in the morning we arrived in St. Louis. We separated at the train yards, as we were from all parts of the city and we would make our way back to camp as best we could. I left at seven o'clock Sunday night but now knew enough to catch a manifest train. Manifests usually carry perishable goods and they travel as fast as passenger trains, making a minimum of stops. I arrived at Poplar Bluff at three minutes to midnight. The camp truck waited at the station until three minutes after twelve but my train went deep into the yards and I hurried back to where the truck normally was, only to see the tail lights disappearing down the road. It was 15 miles back to camp and I had to be there for the morning bugle. I took a short cut through a graveyard, which, though it didn't frighten me, did stir my imagination a bit. I left the cemetery and began to walk on a red gravel road. The only sound was the measured tread of my work boots scuffing the gravel. No moon and the air was still. I suddenly heard footsteps coming towards me. It was as though the steps were trying to keep time with mine. I slowed and the strange footsteps slowed. I stopped and they stopped. I began to walk again and heard them coming closer and closer. I wished I was back in the cemetery—any place where there was a crowd. I started again, and now they were quite close. With a startling suddenness a match was lit and I saw a man's face. He quickly lit a cigarette and then blew the match out, making it seem even darker than before. He laughed with all the charm of Count Dracula and then walked on past me. I still get a shiver up my spine whenever I think of this incident, and I think of all the strange people there are in this world. And I have met a lot of them.

I only saw two cars all through the night, and they didn't give me a lift. I stopped a few times to rest but finally made it to camp with a few minutes to spare. That day I asked a boy working alongside to cover me with branches so I could get some sleep.

The C.C.C. camps were run on army discipline, and just as soldiers got honorable discharges we had to earn the same. I don't know how a dishonorable discharge could hurt you, but being a boy from the reform school I wanted to get out clean. I almost didn't make it, because a great rebellion took place and I was somewhat in the middle. A member of the Corps, working and living on army property, was entitled to three hot meals a day. But each day we'd go a little farther from camp and our noon meal was apt to be on the chilly side. Cold sandwiches were bad enough, but cold stew is impossible. We worked under the direction of a Forestry Supervisor and he paid no attention to the complaints we had made. One boy in particular really knew how to beef loud and strong. His name was Sam Longmeyer, and he stated loud and clear that he wasn't going to work if he had to eat cold slop. The Forestry boss then told us all to make up our minds. All the boys who didn't like the food were to line up on one side of the road and the boys who had no complaints go to the other side.

All the boys went to the complaining side of the road with one exception. But he was to prove to me that I am not the greatest puncher in the world. This boy was effeminate, with a high soprano voice. He was a big lad, with an 18-inch neck and a head to match. He sat there on a log and I felt it was an insult to all his buddies for him to be the only one who didn't protest. I walked over to him and looked at him. He didn't move. I drew my hand back with obvious intentions and he still didn't move. I hit him a solid punch right in the chops and he blinked his eyes and said tearfully, "Why did you do that?"

I could feel the pain running up my arm from my bruised knuckles. If he had made a move I'd have left in a hurry. But I stood there and bluffed him. I said, "Now let that be a lesson to you, and don't make me hit you again." I couldn't have hit him with the brakeman's club. My arm was positively numb. He crossed the road and now we were one hundred percent solid against the Forestry Supervisor. He told us to pile into the trucks and we'd go back to camp and let Captain Parks settle the matter.

Captain Parks called an assembly and began to denounce the organizers of the strike. He pointed out a number of boys and told them they would have to leave camp that day with dishonorable discharges. There were about 200 in all in our group. I had been wanting to leave the C.C.C. but decided to wait a few more weeks until this unpleasantness had died down. I wanted an honorable discharge. My role in the strike was never mentioned, and I think it was because of the fine boxing team I had organized and coached.

Harry Chitwood was a new boy on the scene. He didn't take to our rules very well and was a veritable hawk in the dining room. He'd break line to get into the mess hall first and would never wait his turn to be served food. He could lunge and spear better than the senior Fairbanks. We all resented this kind of behavior, for there was plenty of food for all and we were supposed to be pals. He maintained no one had a right to tell him how to eat. So, one day, I left the table before the meal was over and it looked as though I was going back to the barracks to lie down. I waited just outside the mess hall door and as Chitwood came out I busted him with a hard right hand to the eye. I hit him in his good eye. His other eye was very bad, so with the additional handicap I gave him he couldn't see for a week and depended on all of us to feed him. Naturally he went running to the captain and made a strong protest at my taking over for Emily Post.

Captain Parks heard the story from some of the other boys and he fined me $2 of my monthly 5 and made me keep my hands in my pockets for two weeks when not working or eating. It was hard to do this but I stuck it out, for this was the only trouble I had had in camp and I wanted to get out with a good record. I still hear from Harry Chitwood, and we can now look back on the incident and laugh about it. All this while I was also fighting in the various tournaments, representing the C.C.C. camp. When I decided I wanted to go back to St. Louis I asked Captain Parks for an honorable discharge, which he gave me with his blessings.

Back in St. Louis I was able to get a Federal job that was part-time and paid me $19 a month but I soon switched over to the W.P.A. and was paid $22 a week. In salary I got $14 a week and the rest was made up by "subsistance allowance," which was rice, potatoes and tinned beef, and an occasional clothing allowance. During those days, in my free time, I would walk to the library in downtown St. Louis and read accounts of fights all over the country. I kept on with daily road-work while I was working on the W.P.A.

My first amateur fight was against Raymond Brewster and I won by a knockout in the third round. Then a bantamweight named George Porter became my close friend, and one weekend when I was home from camp he took me to see Monroe Harrison, a boxer, who was interested in Porter's career. Our next step was to see the Kessler brothers, Benny, Solly and Harry. Harry is the well-known metallurgist who became a dilettante referee. Refereeing for fun turned out not to be fun for Archie when Kessler, years later, refereed my fight with Rocky Marciano and stood between me and the champ when I had just stunned him with a right hand. In those days the Kesslers were fight promoters around St. Louis. They entered me in an elimination contest and I boxed a boy named Julius Kemp (A.A.U. champion) and I thought I was giving him a lot of trouble when the fight was stopped. It was explained to me later that Kemp had a fair reputation and would be a better box-office draw, so he got the decision. Kemp went on to win the tournament in the welterweight division.

Again George and I went to Harrison and Benny Kessler. I let Porter do the talking. I had learned at reform school to keep my mouth shut. Porter told them that I was the best amateur welterweight and that he was the best bantamweight. Kessler asked if I was willing to fight Kemp. I said I certainly was. He quickly recapped Kemp's record and asked about mine. I replied I had had no fights of record but he finally agreed to match me. The fight was held at the west side ball park, and I scored a sensational knockout over Kemp in the third round and left him flat on his back. On the same card Porter won his fight by a decision over Hughie Epperson.

The reason for recapping these early fights before I left the C.C.C. camp is that a manager named George Wilsman brought two fighters to Poplar Bluff for a match. He managed Alan Mathews and Benny Deathpane. Deathpane trained just outside Poplar Bluff but Wilson brought Mathews to the C.C.C. camp to train. Naturally my boxing group did all we could to help or just be around this professional. The fight was to be held at the stadium in Poplar Bluff, and Wilson asked Captain Parks if he'd permit the camp trucks to take the boys who wanted to see the fight. Four or five trucks rolled out that evening but the truck with the boxing team was the most excited. We were going to see the great Benny Deathpane and the up-and-coming Alan Mathews.

In the preliminary fights a local boy named Bill Sims, a light-heavy who weighed 169 pounds, fought a boy who looked like he had just jumped off a freight train. The boy more or less quit in the first round and Sims tired of hitting him. The crowd booed the fight, and the C.C.C. boys booed the loudest. Sims made a plea from the ring saying it wasn't his fault, the boy just wouldn't fight. My close pals hollered back, "We got someone to fight you!" I was busy eating popcorn when they turned to me and demanded I fight Sims. I had no equipment with me, but the obliging management dug up a pair of sneakers a size too small and a pair of swimming trunks. I had no protective cup and they gave me a battered pair of gloves. I had been a bit reluctant to go through with this, but the excitement of being in the stadium plus the driving enthusiasm of my buddies made me feel keyed up and anxious to begin. I fought Sims and the contagion of my buddies' confidence gave me an extra incentive. I gave him a bad pounding. I just couldn't stop. They carried him out of the arena and both eyes were closed and he had lost two teeth. I dressed hurriedly to get back and watch Deathpane and Mathews. Mathews beat him with a searing left hook to the body in the fifth round. Deathpane dropped as though shot, but to these people who saw few fights a body-blow knockdown was just not kosher. This was many years before TV, and the opportunity to see live fights were very few for communities like Poplar Bluff. At any rate, not understanding the power of the punch Deathpane had received, the crowd booed and began making catcalls. Once again my dear buddies began to yell for me to fight Mathews. I was only eighteen, and Mathews was a seasoned pro of twenty-two or twenty-three. I had no right to be in a ring with Mathews or even Deathpane right then. Both Mathews and manager George Wilson knew this, and they ignored the crowd. I kept my mouth full of popcorn and said nothing. But when Mathews and Wilson ignored the shouted requests for me to fight, the crowd thought Mathews was afraid of me, and I was then the greatest fighter in the area.

During the last days of my time at the C.C.C. camp a man named Billy Ciscoe became interested in my career. One weekend he took me aside and asked if I would like to make $10. To someone earning $5 a month 10 bucks is a very respectable sum. I was to fight in Hot Springs, Arkansas, and he took me to the Barbara Worth Hotel. We ate in the kitchen, he out of politeness to me and I because the lighting in the white dining room made me look too dark. The food was somewhat better in the kitchen, for we got a lot of extra attention the folks in the other room couldn't afford. It was a fine meal, and I went for a stroll before the fight and saw Tommy Freeman, the ex-welterweight champion, standing outside the firehouse he worked in, with his thumbs hooked through his overalls just like the other farmers standing with him who'd come to town on fight night. The main event was a cross-eyed fighter who used the ring name, Benny Turpin. I remember his name, as he was named for the famous movie comedian, but his opponent's name escapes me. I know it's going to worry you but I can't remember if Turpin won or not, but I often wonder how I'd have fought him. Some boxers watch a man's eyes to foretell where the next punch is being aimed, and with a cross eyed boxer this could be a slight handicap.

I boxed a boy from Fort Smith, Arkansas, called the Pocahontas Kid. He left his tomahawk at home and I scalped him with boxing gloves in two rounds. Billy Ciscoe carefully totaled up the money and deducted the mysterious expenses all managers are born with and then gave me $3. To me it was better than nothing. I was too young to know this was how it was going to be all my life. I had one more fight in Poplar Bluff against Jackie Don Burdin and won in the first round. Soon after that I left the C. C. C. and went back to St. Louis.

After Billy Ciscoe the next man to take an interest (and I do mean *take*) in me was a promoter-matchmaker manager named Kid Bandy. In Mississippi we used to call banty roosters "bandy." The name intrigued me. George Porter introduced me to Bandy, who had a gymnasium upstairs on South Jefferson which was about 3½ miles from where I lived on North Leffenwell Street. The Kid, at that time, had a clever fighter named Joey Parks. He had a good left hand, a good stiff jab and was an in-and-out boxer. In-and-out constantly with that left jab. His punch wasn't much but he made up for it with boxing style, and since I've always admired ring skill more than brawlers with a punch I thought Parks was just about the greatest I'd seen. Bandy put me in to spar with his tiger, and naturally Joe didn't try to hurt me because I was just a green kid and I boxed as nicely and cleverly as I could. Of course Bandy paid me nothing to spar with Joe, as he thought I should have been happy for the opportunity to help Joe get in shape for his fights. But about three weeks after I started with Bandy he got me a fight in Quincy, Illinois, with Speedy Schaefer. Schaefer had fought around St. Louis for some time and in my mind I had built up his skill, which really wasn't there. We fought a six-round draw but Bandy seemed to be satisfied.

Now I was still an amateur fighter. If you won as an amateur you might be given a watch or some other trinket which you could sell right back to the promoter, and that was how you'd make a little money and retain your amateur standing. Kid Bandy knew that as long as I was an amateur other managers would be interested in me, so, in order to kill that danger, he put me on a variety card promoted by Larry Atkins featuring Bobby Breen and Fifi D'Orsay with several Hollywood acts plus a feature wrestling bout. There were two boxing bouts with Joey Parks fighting on the main event and I fought Charley Dawson. Since it was an entertainment feature we merely went through the motions in more of an exhibition of boxing than a bout itself. Bandy gave me $3 for this. Immediately someone informed the A.A.U. that I had been paid by Bandy and they picked up my amateur's license. That ended any hope I had had for an Olympic title. It forced me to turn professional, but the commission was very compassionate and gave me a professional license after hearing what I had been paid for appearing on that variety card.

By getting a professional license for $3 instead of $5 I was ahead of the fight game by $2 when I began. I haven't really been ahead since. I was now on the W.P.A. and my family, like everyone around us, was on relief. I used to play a little dice with the boys. Mostly I lost, but was careful to keep my losings to my share of my salary, turning the rest over to Auntie to support the family. But one day I got hooked in a game in which a sharpie switched crooked dice into the game, and lost my entire salary. That following week was one of the most miserable. If you can learn a lesson the hard way, I did, as I don't gamble at all anymore and haven't any desire to. That week was navy beans and Argentine beef every meal. And the silence around the table was all pointed at me.

Each gang on the W.P.A. had a boss. He got $2 more than we did, and that $2 changed many a man from a mouse into a cowardly lion. One cold day we were repairing a levee and it was mighty cold outdoors. We had a fire going and there was a lull in the work as we had to tear down tarpaper shacks put up by poor folks who had no other place to live. Until they moved out we just couldn't demolish their homes. So it went slow, with eight men pulling down a shack the big, bad wolf could have knocked over with a sneeze. The temperature was about two above zero and we had a nice fire going in an old garbage can when this boss came by. He told us to kick out the fire. No one moved. He pointed at me and gave me a direct order but I ignored him. He said he was going on an inspection tour and when he returned the fire had better be out. He was gone less than five minutes and then said if we didn't kick the fire out he'd give someone a 403. A 403 meant dismissal, and dismissal meant curtains in those days, for there were no jobs to be had and the W.P.A. was rock bottom. No one moved; the fire crackled warmly as we leaned on our shovels and picks. He pushed us aside and kicked the fire, over. I got so incensed I threw my shovel up in the air and said that settled it. I was quitting and going to become a professional fighter twenty-four hours a day. I was sick of living like this and knew that unless I finally took the bit in my teeth I would never amount to more than a preliminary club fighter. I walked away from the job with the good wishes of an old man ringing in my ears. The others, quite naturally, thought I was crazy to quit, and I certainly knew my auntie would agree with them.

Before I continue with my saga of fight managers I have known I would like to set down on the record what actually happened in a fight I had with Frankie Nelson. I was accused of quitting in the ring. Today, with a long history of fights behind me and more than twenty years of active campaigning, I believe that record states I am not a quitter. Nor was I then. I greatly admired a boy named Monroe Harrison, and he coached me in his style of fighting, which you can call the shell technique. With both hands cocked in front of you it affords an excellent defense, while it enables you to pop or explode a punch with either hand without any telltale shoulder movement. The style I use today is a further perfection of what Monroe taught me many years ago. This tournament fight was held in Cleveland, and we fought with our own sportswriter covering for St. Louis. He was Mr. Bill McCoogan of the St. Louis *Post-Dispatch.* Frankie Nelson was an aggressive fighter, and my shell style worked fine, except I could only use it as a defense. But to anyone at ringside it appeared as though I was covering my face in sheer terror and taking the punches and praying for the bell to save me. Mr. McCoogan believed I had just quit. I was praying all right, praying for one opening in this windmill I was facing. The boy had four arms that night. But there I was, in the shell and moving around the ring, and it must have seemed the same to the referee, for he stopped the fight thinking I was hurt. I wasn't, but they don't allow curtain speeches in the ring. McCoogan printed what he thought and it was quite a while before I could live that fight down, although years later McCoogan acknowledged the style was a good one, even though I didn't display it to the best advantage against Frankie Nelson. That was in 1936 in the National Amateur Tournament held in Cleveland.

After Kid Bandy came George Wilsman. He had quite a stable of fighters and a wonderful knack of making money for George Wilsman. A sportswriter once said of me, "Archie Moore is a great guide. He can lead you to wherever he wants to go." I think that applies equally well to Wilsman. Here's one incident that happened.

Wilsman matched me to fight a boy in Ponca City, Oklahoma, and on the same card Wilsman had two of his other fighters, Alan Mathews and Merle Thompson. I won in two rounds. I was promised $35. Wilsman was matchmaker and manager. He controlled the fighters and the expense end of it. When we returned he gave me $12. The W.P.A. was far better than that.

Shortly after this I met Cal Thompson. He lived in Indianapolis. He came back to my dressing room after I scored a victory, and he truly had the gift of gab. He had true flash. A smooth dresser with a glib style of speech and mannerisms, he certainly looked successful, and I was flattered and said to myself this must be a terrific man. He asked me how many fights I had had and was surprised to hear how few. We were talking, naturally, of professional fights, and at that time I'd only had six or seven. Prior to this fight I hadn't fought in three months, and when Thompson said he could get me all the fights I wanted I mentally said goodbye to Wilsman on the spot and added another mentor to my growing list. I was willing to take his word for anything he said. This has always been my undoing. I was so anxious to continue fighting I grabbed at straws, even when they were gilt-edged like Cal. I had to earn money or stop fighting. It was as simple as that.

I listened openmouthed to this golden orator who spun dreams of wealth and fame, and he concluded by inviting me to his home for a late sandwich. The first thing that impressed me was his fine car, the current year's model, a sleek 1937 Dodge, and it looked twice as big and twice as beautiful as it actually was because it was black and had two spotlights and white-wall tires and was shined to a high gloss. Then we arrived at his house and in the dark it looked like a mansion to me. The inside of the house amazed me. He had a grand piano in his huge living room, three bedrooms and a dining room and kitchen. Most amazing, he had two bathrooms! I had never been in anybody's home with a bathroom inside, and to have two was overdoing it, to say the least.

I wasn't old enough to sign a contract, so I had no legal obligation to Thompson or Wilsman. But Thompson seemed to be the man to be with and I told him I'd like him to handle me. My verbal agreement with Wilsman meant nothing, since he'd only gotten me one fight in the last three months. I didn't feel at all disloyal.

My mother was back living with us and she was working. She was supporting the family at this time, but they all had hopes that I would get the right break and come through as a big breadwinner. I was willing.

The very first night we met Cal suggested I move in with him, as that would keep my expenses down. It was a good idea to me, since I wouldn't have to eat at home and money saved was money earned. The next morning I ate my first piece of toast made in a toaster, and thereby hangs a tale. My auntie used to butter a slice of bread and heat it on the stove, and that was toast as I knew it. But watching Mrs. Thompson make toast really intrigued me, so when the kids went off to school and Cal left to open his downtown barber shop and Mrs. Thompson went to her dress shop, I was ready for action. I took out a loaf of bread and got some butter from the icebox. I spread butter on two slices and popped them into the toaster. I buttered the bread first just as Auntie did. I ate a whole loaf of fine toasted bread. But the butter had just about ruined the toaster, and Mrs. Thompson wanted me out of the house almost before I moved in. What really did it, though, was the fact that I would get up hours before the rest to do my roadwork, and the noise of me bustling about the kitchen making a cup of coffee or tea or whatever before I left woke up various members of the household and she persuaded her husband to make other arrangements for me. Cal moved me into a boardinghouse run by Mrs. Lee Pretriman, and it suited me fine, for Mrs. Pretriman cooked some of the best meals I have ever eaten since I left home.

I had seven fights in nine months and was feeling pretty good. I had a girl at that time, Gladys Walker, and I thought I was in love. I know that I was very, very fond of Gladys and I used to walk many, many blocks in all kinds of weather to see her. She was indifferent at the beginning of our attachment, but as I started to hang up a string of victories she warmed considerably. My entertainment costs weren't high as you could go to a dance for 50 or 75 cents and hear a fine band for that money in those days. I didn't smoke or drink and didn't care much for girls who did drink so I could go out with $2.50 and have a fine time.

Cal Thompson got me a trainer, Hiawatha Grey. On and off through the years Hiawatha has been in my corner, including my last fight with Durelle. I have known him since 1937. He smoothed my rough edges, curbed my eagerness and made me think like a professional instead of a hungry kid out to make a name for himself.

But outside the ring I was still a hungry kid who wanted recognition, and I met a man named Felix Thurman who proposed we pick up stakes and go to California where a fresh name could get fights. Since the West Coast was great for fighting it might just be that Archie Moore could come into his own out there. Gladys and I were still friends but had cooled off, and I was restless to shake loose from familiar surroundings and see what I could do away from home. George Porter needled me, saying the West Coast fighters like Swede Berglund and Bandit Romero would take me apart. The more he needled the more I listened to Felix. He was sending his wife and daughter on ahead and would sell his small garage to finance our trip West. He was an expert mechanic, which is as good a qualification for a fight manager as any I can think of. I resolved to leave Cal Thompson and Hiawatha and head West. At the time, it would have surprised me if I'd known I'd get as far west as Tasmania. At any rate, the days of $ 5 a month were over, because without knowing it I had been living on nothing but hot air for some weeks.

# ROUND 3 I HEAR YOU, MR. GREELEY!

Neither Felix nor I was afraid of Indians but we had a great respect for the desert. We stocked our car with soft drinks, apples and bags of peanuts. Eating peanuts in a desert will make you look for water all the more. I had no trepidations about Felix making the car perform; he could have kept it going on three wheels. He had all his expensive mechanic's tools in the back and our personal belongings were heaped on the rear seat.

On March 29, 1938, towards dusk, we were heading for Texas through Oklahoma. Down the road a car trying to pass another swung into our lane. A head-on crash could only be avoided by our leaving the road. Off we went and over the car turned. The grass was slippery from irrigation which overran the highway shoulder and it flipped the car, knocking us both unconscious. I came to first, and all I could hear in the ominous silence was a steady drip, drip, drip. Gas! I scrambled to open the door and get out, but with the car upside down I was tugging the handle the wrong way and it wouldn't open. I thought it was jammed and began kicking at the window. I cracked it and then, in impatience, I relied on a straight right jab, which broke through the window but almost severed the artery in the right wrist. I managed to get out and discovered the dripping was water from the wheels, which were still turning. I staggered backwards and fell into a flooded ditch beside the road. I lost both my shoes but managed to get around the car and pull Felix from behind the steering wheel. I realized I had panicked from fear of fire and explosion but now was fairly calm, although the dreadful bleeding was beginning to set me off again.

A 1938 Oldsmobile pulled up, and in it were two internes and two student nurses. "Lucky we came by," one interne said. "Arterial bleeding is fatal in fourteen minutes."

The control of fear is something everyone should try. I mean the wild fear that occurs in a crisis. A police officer I know, Junior Washington, once ran to an exploded gasoline truck and pulled the driver from the burning cab, getting severely burned himself by doing so. I asked him some time later if he hadn't been afraid of another explosion and certain death. He said he was aware of it in the back of his mind, but his sole concern at the time was to get the poor devil out of the cab. His fear during that crisis was controlled. As a fighter I feel a certain amount of fear every time I get in a ring. I wouldn't be human if I didn't. But the first punch is the only one I really feel. Just as a fighter knows he is going to be hit, the ordinary person in a crisis can quickly define his fear and lick it. My panic at the jammed door was unwarranted. The result of that panic almost caused my death. I have tried, ever since, to control my emotions about injury, illness or family emergencies.

After applying a tourniquet and after Felix rounded up both my shoes they told me to get into the car. I refused, as it was a brand-new car and I was a mess. I was in a state of shock. I can remember names of fighters I've fought and hundreds I haven't fought but I can't remember one name of any of those kind, humane and wonderful people. Felix stood by silently as the two internes ranged on both sides of me and tugged me towards the back seat. They motioned for Felix to join us, and I wrapped myself in a topcoat and pondered on fate. Having this turn of events follow a near-tragic accident was almost too much for me to comprehend. I had grown to expect that any car, in Oklahoma, seeing two Negro men overturned in a ditch, would ride on, probably commenting on what bad moonshine we must have drunk and never giving us a further thought. Yet within minutes a car stopped, the first car indeed that had come along, and, miracle of miracles, it contained people able and willing to give me instant medical attention. I don't know whether God is a white man or a black man but I had to realize in that moment, He had truly made us all.

Upon arrival at the hospital my basic fears returned. No matter how kind the internes and nurses were I was worried about how I would be received in the hospital. This is part and parcel of being a colored man in the South—and, for the most part, in the North, too. Again my fears were groundless. A very sympathetic doctor treated my wrist and assured me that if I had it checked as soon as I arrived in California, I would have full movement of my hands and wrist. Many readers will not understand how deep my gratitude went, but part of it was due to shame for feeling hurt where no hurt was ever intended. But it is the hurt that happens when a Negro is off guard that cements the barrier often felt by white people who have no prejudice and are puzzled when rebuffed after a friendly overture.

The doctor was a fight fan but had not heard of me. In particular, like so many people in those days, he was a Joe Louis fan. Although I never met Joe then, I had enough knowledge of fighting and of the fighters Louis had fought to talk intelligently to him. Felix had gone to order a tow truck, and I left the hospital glowing with warmth and walked to the garage to wait for him.

The car was all right except for a dented top and the window I had broken. Felix got his mallet and straightened the top by himself. We had left St. Louis with a total of $40 and the tow job cost $12. We bought two containers of coffee and drove off sipping quietly, both of us thinking of what had happened. The doctor had said I should eat some food and drink some milk to balance the loss of blood, but as I was young and strong as an ox I believed sitting in the car would renew my strength, and we needed every penny for gas.

As we rolled into Amarillo Felix confessed he had to see a dentist. All the while I had been silently enduring my weak feeling he had been fighting the gnawing pain of a toothache. The dentist pulled the tooth—$5, please. Gasoline prices got higher as we went West. We finally ran out of money in Grant's, New Mexico, and Felix called his wife collect in La Jolla to send money. Although Felix's wife was working I doubt if she was making more than $14 a week and had her daughter to support, and yet she sent $10. When we left St. Louis we were paying 15 cents a gallon for gas and it was now costing 34 cents and higher. We reached Flagstaff, Arizona, and were practically broke again. So far we had had an orange each, two Cokes, two containers of coffee and some apples. Felix tightened the gas jet soon after pawning most of his expensive tools. With a full tank of gas and a slower flow we had to travel at much less speed and it was a toss-up whether to conserve gas and starve or go full blast and pray. On our tank of gas, plus coasting down the Rockies for 13 miles (ruined the brakes), we managed to reach San Bernardino, which was about 100 miles from Felix's home. No gas and no tools left to pawn. Felix rummaged around and came up with a spray gun, and a garage man gave us a tank of gas for it. We finally arrived at the beautiful town of La Jolla about three in the morning and I stretched out for the first time after the most exhausting trip I had ever made. The Pacific was right outside my door. I was West. Now what?

I was fortunate in one respect. It seemed a privilege to live in La Jolla, the Jewel City. A fabulous resort town with lovely beaches and a wonderful climate. It is actually a peninsula, and you can see far up the coast or back into the Coronado Islands. I did my early morning roadwork on the beach and Felix, wanting to know as much as he could about boxing, came with me one day and we raced for a hundred yards or so. I gave Felix a head start and he beat me by a step or two. I challenged him to race back and he strained his heart. It's bothered him ever since. He's the only manager who ever was broken-hearted over Archie Moore.

Felix had the name of a promoter in San Diego, a few miles south of La Jolla, and we were to look him up the day after we arrived. Even though we had turned in after three in the morning, habit woke me at my usual early hour, and I jogged along the beach feeling sure

I had made the right move in leaving St. Louis to come out here. On my return I noticed a huge pall of smoke hovering over San Diego. When I got back to Felix's house he was fixing breakfast and I told him about it. He shrugged and had as much interest as I did. A fire in a totally strange city meant nothing to us. I looked at the neat duplex apartment Mrs. Thurman had rented and ate a fine breakfast and felt contented. She was doing day work for some families who lived in the area, and since most were generous and wealthy our larder was always full. Felix and I straightened up the house and left to find Mr. Platner. What we found was the fire we had seen earlier. It was the Coliseum where the fights were held! Mr. Platner was burned out of business that morning and so was I.

# ROUND 4 SAN DIEGO AND THE BANDIT

The Coliseum was located at 15th and E Streets in San Diego. Cat-a-corner from it was a saloon owned by George Wilson where you could get a bowl of beans or a steak at a reasonable price. His place was the authentic hangout for fighters, managers and, I suppose, bookmakers. It was a part of the romantic days of California boxing in the late twenties and in the thirties. The habitues included such fighters as Young Dado, Dick Ramey, Charles Firaschi, Long Tom Hawkins and Johnny Romero, whose ring nickname was The Bandit.

Linn Platner was the boxing promoter in San Diego. I never figured out what nationality Mr. Platner was, but he was American-born, about forty-five, on the stout side and always well-dressed in a conservative manner. He had a swarthy complexion and a pleasant smile, and was then married to a wonderful woman who passed away later on. He remarried and now lives in a lovely mansion with his wife and child. Mr. Platner was an influential citizen in San Diego and took an interest in civic affairs. The Coliseum was an important building in the city and was much in demand for other events beside fight cards.

When Felix and I entered Wilson's saloon and inquired about Mr. Platner he immediately stood up and shook hands with us. I sensed right away that Mr. Platner's interest was in fighters and the sport. Money was secondary. He was and is unique in the fight game. I expected him to show some emotion over the disaster across the street which was still smoldering but he had an affable business-as-usual manner. He suggested we step outside for our talk, for the saloon office was too small to hold us and the ears inside were too numerous to count. Now, I am a great sidewalk talker. I can talk Mexican fashion squatting on my heels, or big-city style with my spine against a lamppost or building, and even garment-center technique with my backside defying traffic at the edge of the curb. I found Platner more on the latter style and admired his aplomb as fire and police equipment brushed past him and he never dropped a syllable. I suddenly realized how tired I was, and sank down to a fashionable Laredo squat as Platner and Thurman spoke together. They were getting along like two flies at a free lunch counter when suddenly Platner nudged me with a number 11 shoe and said, "Can you fight?"

Now, I knew he wasn't being facetious but was waiting to see what kind of answer he'd get, to find out if he was talking to a fresh kid or a man. I answered quietly, "I think I can."

Mr. Platner smiled and said, "That's what I want. Not a fighter who has to be babied along. You've had sixteen fights, but most of them have been prelims or in small clubs. Not main events. Do you think you can handle a main event?"

I smiled back at him. "Mr. Platner," I said, "I thought that's what you meant by the first question." You see, down deep I *was* a fresh kid.

Now Platner explained to me and Felix that he intended to continue promoting while the Coliseum was being rebuilt. He was going to lease Lane Field. It was situated about a half block from the 11th Naval District Warehouse. It was a small park that seated about 10,000.

His first card for the outdoor promotion starred the ex-light-heavyweight champion of the world, Maxie Rosenbloom, versus

Odell Pollee, a young colored boy from Philadelphia currently living in San Francisco. It was held on May 20, 1938. The rest of the card had been filled out with the exception of the semifinal, and Platner asked if I would box against a young fellow from Hollywood named Jimmy Brent. He was a prospect, as they say on Jacob's Beach, but like a lot of prospecting he didn't pan out. In one minute and forty-five seconds of the first round Jimmy was flat on his back listening to the count of ten. I bundled up in my robe and was amazed to hear Mr. Platner announce to the crowd that I would be back in the ring the following week. I stayed in my robe to watch Rosenbloom fight Pollee. I wanted to see an ex-champ in action. I was amazed at Rosenbloom's lack of ability, though I must say he had lost the title a long time before. He merely slapped Pollee around the ring and the referee kept making Pollee rise from these slap-downs.

In my mind I was making preparations to ask Platner for a match with Rosenbloom. He could slap all he wanted to, I intended to punch. In the dressing room I was beaming inwardly. I thought I now had a chance to get a lot of fights, make a regional name for myself and eventually become known to sports writers all over the country. The young editors in San Diego at that time were not much older than I was. In a body they cried out in horror. Is this for real? Did this man Moore really punch so hard and so fast? But the wise old owl Mr. Tom Akers, sports editor of the *Evening Tribune*, said he'd seen potential greatness, and surely young Archie Moore had more to show.

I suppose that many athletes who rise in their field and just as many actors who gain fame in their profession cherish the early encouraging notices more than any others. Luckily I have been well treated by the press, and hereby acknowledge my appreciation. In later years they took many of my statements tongue-in-cheek, but they never ridiculed my skills and for that I thank them, one and all.

Platner kept his word but my dream didn't come true. I fought the following week but by then Slapsie Maxie had gone. I was matched with Ray Vargas, a young Mexican from Anaheim,

California. Vargas had a noisy manager named Johnny Kell of who demanded I take off one more pound at the weighing-in, as I had come in overweight at 161. I calmly took a package of chewing gum from my pocket and fed myself slice after slice until I had the whole gob going like a working cud. I chewed and spit, chewed and spit. I did the contented cow scene for a half hour and then stepped on the scales and weighed in at exactly 160 pounds. Later the same day, without gum, I chewed up Ray Vargas in a fancy three-round knockout. Mr. Platner's eyes did have a glazed look, but it was the only time I could see dollar signs in them when he blinked. He was profuse in his congratulations and mumbled about a shortage of good fighters even in those days of "live" fight cards. He said further that the fans were demanding to know whether I was really a good fighter or just a flash in the pan. Before I could follow the path he was laying out he asked me if I thought I was good enough to fight The Bandit, and I replied in my most modest and positive manner, "Try me!"

Johnny "The Bandit" Romero had fought most of the better West Coast fighters. Men like Ceferino Garcia, Gorilla Jones, former middleweight champion, and Swede Berglund, who had been a rated middleweight in his time. He was a southpaw fighter, a terrific puncher, but was considered and in-and-outer by the boxing crowd. At times he'd turn in a performance of championship caliber and at other times he'd louse up a fight card beyond repair. The Bandit was sure he could beat young Archie Moore. He was then twenty-seven years old, and the fight critics believe a man of that age to be going downhill. I have never quite agreed with that theory.

The Rosenbloom versus Pollee fight had drawn 1100 people. The main event between Moore and The Bandit drew 3500 people. My popularity after the win over Vargas plus The Bandit's built-in fans was responsible for the turnout. I had received a $95 purse for my end after the Vargas fight and got the tremendous sum of $195 for fighting Romero. I had gotten $35 for the Brent fight, and so my total take since I'd been in San Diego was $276. Actually this was earned in one month. This money, naturally, was shared with Felix

Thurman. We had to eat, sleep, train and amuse ourselves on $69 a week split between us. I point this out to make it understandable to the public that when a fighter does gain prominence he has a right to hold out for big paydays. (There! And I'll bet you thought I'd never say anything nice about Sugar Ray Robinson.)

At the weigh-in I scaled 159 and the Bandit tipped the balance bar at 167. I didn't think boxing a southpaw would present any particular difficulty, as I had a left jab that I planned to keep in his face all night. I took charge of the fight at the outset and boxed rings around him for three full rounds. He was so busy defending himself I doubt if he threw more than five punches. In the fourth, I decided to set him up for the kill and was throwing fast punches to keep him off balance and to allow me to put together a good combination, but for a split second I did forget Romero was a southpaw and his left hand clipped me solidly and I found myself sitting in a corner, dazed and hurt. Felix, inexperienced as he was, had rushed around the ring apron and was holding me down to take a count and rest. Why no one tried to disqualify me for that I'll never know. The Mexican fans were screaming at the colored fans and the place was in a complete uproar. At the count of eight Felix let go of my trunks and I sprang up. Through a glaze I saw The Bandit coming for me and all I could see was that big left hand and I ducked. I ducked enough to avoid a direct hit but he struck me a glancing blow on the temple and down I went for the second time. I had more command of my faculties now and I got up at the count of eight. The bell rang and I went to my corner. That's all I can recall.

At the beginning of the eighth round Felix broke a stick of aromatic spirits of ammonia under my nose and my vision cleared and I suddenly remembered where I was. I asked Felix if the fight was over and he said no. He told me it was the eighth round. I asked if I had won the first three and when he said yes I realized The Bandit had won the next four. With rounds eight, nine and ten coming up I still had a chance to win.

It was as though the fight was just beginning. Years later, in my first fight with Durelle, I had almost the same feeling. I raced off the stool to intercept The Bandit. I met him in his own corner and laid my head against his chest and began pummeling his body, and I stayed that way until the end of the round. I continued the same tactics until the end of the fight and The Bandit was certainly happy when the end came. Doubly so, for the referee who was the sole judge in those days, raised his hand in victory and, as he announced his decision, bedlam broke loose in the arena. My fans were enraged because of my comeback in the last three rounds. His fans were jubilant and goading all the losers. The desperate turn-about run I had made should have given me six rounds against four for Romero. The referee's decision couldn't or wouldn't be changed. I thought the wrong guy in the ring was nicknamed The Bandit. Then the fans began throwing bottles, and as I had one eye completely swollen shut and the other was closing fast I was in more danger from flying bottles than when I had been in the ring with Romero. I am a firm believer in paper cups and soft, soft drinks.

Physically I was in very good shape. I looked a mess and I certainly knew I had been in a fight, but the applause of the fans was quite heartening as I walked up the aisle to the dressing room. But the clamor didn't quite ease my disappointment, because I firmly believed I could have knocked the Bandit out and inwardly I was raging because I hadn't done so. I stalled in the dressing room to let the crowd disperse, as it is always embarrassing to walk out a loser among people who have faith in you and money riding on you. You can believe me when I say a fighter doesn't fight just for money. The night Joe Louis lost to Max Schmeling he felt ashamed to walk through the streets of Harlem, but when he was finally persuaded to, the reception he got from his loyal fans forged his determination to beat the German in the rematch. Patterson, too, after losing his title to Johansson, stayed in his home for days with the shades drawn. A Negro champion feels he stands for more than just a title. He is a symbol of achievement and dignity and it is tough to be a loser and let a whole race down. This is not saying that life is as simple as white versus black, as I am quite sure great white fighters take as much pride in winning as I do and feel just as bad when they lose. The fighting game is now a true democracy, and it is just a question of who can beat whom. But on this night, sitting in the dressing room, I was the representative of the Negroes versus the Mexicans and I didn't want to go out among them. About an hour had passed when a sportswriter knocked on the door of the dressing room and stuck his head in.

"Archie," he said, "come on outside. There are hundreds of people waiting on you."

I couldn't believe him, and yet I surely wanted to. Timidly I went outside. I certainly didn't want to collect the deposit on thrown bottles. It was the first time I had been among such a crowd as Archie Moore the fighter. This was a crowd who had just seen me fight and waited to see me leave the arena. They swarmed around me, white, colored and Mexican and all screaming to heaven for justice, saying I had won the fight. Right then and there they initiated a petition demanding Archie Moore and The Bandit in a rematch. At the time I couldn't have fought a soft, round girl, but that bunch of people did make me feel like a winner.

Felix and I were still living in La Jolla, where I was teaching Sunday school for Reverend Blackmore in our local Presbyterian Church, and everyone, especially the kids, made it a point to tell me they thought I had won the fight. The newspapers got on the bandwagon and Platner convinced Romero. The rematch was set for a Fall date and the Coliseum was being rebuilt and would be ready. As soon as my eyes had healed (I'm a fanatic about being able to see my opponent), I fought Johnny Sykes, a veteran from Fargo, and won in one round. Next was Lorenzo Pedro, former holder of the State Light Heavyweight Championship. He weighed 171 and I was still a trim 159. I beat him unmercifully for ten rounds and won by unanimous decision.

Then it was time for The Bandit again. The promoters wanted us both to go to the *Tribune* for the weighing-in ceremony, where publicity pictures would be made. We shared a makeshift dressing room there as we changed from street clothes to our fighting uniforms.

While we were changing, The Bandit confided in me, saying he had fought several colored fighters and he had a particular warmth for colored fighters. He added that he actually bore no grievance to any man because of race or religion. I got the idea he was trying to give me some sort of racial pitch, seeing as how we were both considered in minority groups. But I cut him off by saying, "Johnny, if I was fighting my brother I'd try to knock him out. And the fact is, Johnny, you are not even my brother, so I'm sure gonna try and knock you out, which I think I can do." My confidence had a sobering effect on Johnny. We posed for pictures and made the usual statements of how we were each going to win, shook hands cordially and went our separate ways. The night of the fight the arena had about 3000 people and I felt fine. The first punch was landed by The Bandit and it almost sickened me. It was a shot in the stomach that seemed to pass right through me, but Johnny was fighting a cautious fight and he had a lot of respect for his colored friend, so instead of moving in for a finish he backed off, not knowing how badly I had been hit. I got on my bike and rode around while my trainer, an old-timer named Sailor Larry, told me to keep moving. Just before the end of the round I had regained enough strength and landed a short right-hand chop that decked him, and for the next four rounds he was my cousin. I beat him back and forth and seemed to land whenever I felt like it, and in the sixth I knocked him down again. In the eighth I saw that big left hand that had been my undoing once before, but this time I stepped inside with a down ward right-hand chop and left Johnny and his left hand flat on the canvas. The arena exploded. I have fought many fights myself, seen countless others, and I have studied the varied styles of boxing. My big conclusion, all other skills being equal, is that in this game you have to be a finisher. If Yvon Durelle had been a finisher he would have won my title in our first fight in Montreal. My second fight with Durelle was a better example of what I mean by a finisher. When you've set your man up for a knockout you must be able to swarm all over him, hitting him time and time again and literally battering him to the floor. Not wild punches but a methodical, one, two, three and four and then over again. Johansson demonstrated this when he won the title from Patterson. To many fans it looks as though a fighter engaged in finishing is just throwing punches, but usually the opponent's loss of control causes him to stagger and reel, thereby unconsciously ducking a lot of jabs and hooks. When Patterson got up from his first knockdown his back was to Johansson. Ingemar cuffed him on the side of the head, with the force of the blow coming from the wrist. This turned Patterson around in savage fashion and he was wide open for Johansson's finishing touches. I've seen many excellent fighters, but the only ones I would bank on would have to be finishers. Without that ability you just aren't cut out to be a fighter. In Dempsey's day they used to call it the killer instinct. I call it finishing, and you don't learn it at Miss Hewitt's School for Young Ladies.

The second Romero fight gave me a new dimension. He was well enough known to gain me recognition for having beaten him. I felt I was made as a fighter, as I would now be known from coast to coast.

I was anxious to pay a visit to St. Louis now that I had scored such a sensational win and had piled up a very-decent record in San Diego. I wanted to gloat a little over my victories to George Porter, since he had said the company on the Coast would be too fast for me. And I wanted to visit Auntie and throw some nice green greeting cards on the table.

So I went back, had my day in the sun and felt mighty pleased. In November and December of 1938 I fought twice in St. Louis and scored a two-round knockout in each fight against Ray Lyle and Irish Bob Turner. It cemented my new reputation and brought me attention in the St. Louis sports pages. Through this I met an insurance man, Mr. Edley Byron Shipman. He and his wife, daughter and son-in-law lived in St. Louis. Mr. Shipman wanted to become a fight manager because his son-in-law, Paul Duke, was a handsome, strapping lad who liked to fight. A Li'l Abner-type boy. He was a heavyweight of amateur status and had fought Louis Q. Murray, one of St. Louis' better heavyweights. He needed tutelage, and Mr. Shipman felt that if he could handle me he'd have a name fighter plus a teacher for his protege. This was early in 1939, and Mr. Shipman wanted to develop Paul as one of the white hopes people were trying to find to get the heavyweight title. I had no qualms about training a white hope, for no matter what color you were you sure needed hope to beat Joe Louis in 1939.

I explained to Shipman that Felix Thurman held my contract and before I could go with him he'd have to settle with Felix. I had two years to go on that contract but the California Boxing Commission favored releasing a fighter from a contract if the manager had not gotten him any fights in four months. I wrote Felix telling him I was going to New York with Shipman and Duke and said goodbye to my family, once again ready to leave St. Louis but this time in the opposite direction.

We took George Porter with us and drove in my Oldsmobile to New York. En route a coal truck slammed into the back of our car and knocked the body out of line. The front seat was off the rack and the back of the car was crushed in but it was a fun trip all the same, as we were looking forward to big things in New York and the truck hadn't killed us.

We arrived in New York and Shipman began to look for a place where we could all stay together. We were finally integrated in a lovely apartment on 110th Street overlooking the northern end of Central Park. A lady named Eloise rented us two rooms, one for Paul and Mr. Shipman, and George and I had the other. Shipman had given me sums of money from time to time and he augmented this with $500 more when I consented to come East, box for him and train his son-in-law. I was riding high.

The food was good and we were near the Pioneer Gymnasium where I taught Paul and did my own working-out. I worked out with an old-timer named Billy Jones, a light heavyweight out of

Philadelphia who had been an excellent boxer and had fought in Australia. But at this time I was twenty-two and he had had it. I was still a middleweight but such a vicious puncher that I gave him the blues in our workouts. I also worked out with Heywood Storey, who was reputed to have once knocked down Joe Louis in a workout. And there was Eddie Mader, who had fought Louis and Galento. But I was making a mistake a more experienced manager than Shipman would have changed. I was fighting too well in the gymnasiums. I was getting a reputation as a very hard puncher. I'd become known as a "spoiler" in the fight business. To other fighters this didn't matter much, but to their managers and trainers it meant a lot. If they were grooming a boy, moving him along, they didn't want him to fight me and have his career spoiled with one fight. I outclassed them and the managers avoided me. Years later Johansson was criticized for "secret" training and not throwing his right hand in sparring bouts. I think he had the right idea, because a lot of my trouble in getting fights stemmed from those foolish days in the Pioneer Gym when my youth prevented me from holding back and I looked too good.

Mr. Shipman was anxious to get me with Mr. Bill Duffy, the man who had managed Primo Camera, the former World's Heavyweight Champ. About the time he was trying to arrange this I fought Paul Duke in an exhibition at the New York World's Fair along with Fred Apostoli and others. George Porter fought on the card, too. Mr. Duffy and Shipman couldn't get together on terms, although Mr. Duffy was anxious to handle me. He took me out one night and we went to the Cotton Club where Cab Calloway was playing and a girl named Lena Horne was in the show. It was the first time, too, I had seen the Nicholas Brothers in person. Bill Robinson was headlining the show and he did a dance for me and Calloway asked what I would like to hear and he played Dinah for me. I had a dish of ice cream and a Coca-Cola and my end of the tab was a dollar-fifty, which Mr. Duffy gladly paid. Can you imagine that? A dollar-fifty for a Coke and an ice cream. In 1939! Boy, I knew I was in New York.

Meanwhile a deal was shaping up for me to go to Australia. The people interested thought I was in San Diego, but a man named Jack Richardson assured every one that he would locate me. Richardson called me and asked me to return to San Diego because he had my ticket for Australia and everything was set. Bill Duffy gave me $30 and George Porter and I loaded our luggage and drove back to St. Louis in twenty-eight hours, non-stop. Upon arriving there, I found a train ticket to California waiting for me, and off I went.

Felix now wanted out on my contract and we had a hearing of our own. Richardson offered Thurman $250, which he accepted, and now Richardson was my manager and at the time it suited me fine. I felt he was aggressive and 100 percent for his fighter. My last fight in America before I left was with Shorty Hogue, and I lost in six rounds. I didn't care; a new continent beckoned me and things looked rosy.

# ROUND 5 CAPTAIN KANGAROO

Being a normal male of sound mind and body, I had always dated girls when my schedule allowed. And being young and interested, I dated girls when my schedule didn't allow. My big romance in the latter part of 1939 was a San Diego girl named Mattie Chapman. I felt I had a career ahead of me and knew I was established as a fighter in San Diego and thought I was now ready for matrimony. We were in love and decided to get married on New Year's Day, 1940. Her brother Earl and her sister Louise and a friend named Ben Merritt accompanied us. We drove from San Diego to Yuma and as we went along we made many stops on Highway 80, all of us in high spirits, and life ahead looked sweet and cool like a fresh-cut melon in the evening. We finally stopped on the other side of El Centro, where they were building the All-American Canal. We found a justice of the peace and were married and drove back to San Diego the same night.

I now had a new wife and a new manager. I thought of the wonderful honeymoon on the long voyage to Australia before starting to train in the land of kangaroos. But Richardson bluntly told me I couldn't take my wife. He took his wife and young son, Mickey, and I couldn't understand any of this. But he now held my contract and I was still quite green in the ways of the world, so I promised Mattie I would send for her as soon as my end of my purses made it possible. My bride of three days bid me a tearful goodbye in

San Pedro when the Matson liner *Monterey* sailed. I had a bottomless feeling in my heart when Mattie's brother escorted her down the gang plank for the drive back to San Diego. Mattie later discovered, as she wrote me in letters, that the Australian expense money had included passage for my trainer, and Richardson had used that ticket for his wife and had then bought a half-fare ticket for Mickey. What was done was done, so I said nothing, but I had been stung again and this time before we had really gotten started as a team.

After all, I was a young fighter with not too much formal education and my knowledge of business was scanty. I avoided most business arrangements and signed papers when and where I was told to with blind faith in the men who guided my boxing destiny. Many years before, Hiawatha Grey had told me to beware, and now his advice was ringing true. I had always placed my confidence in those people who promised to do things for me, but I've long since found out that none of them has ever returned that confidence. As the years went by I realized how boxers are exploited, both white and Negro, and I geared my way of living and my boxing style to outlast most of them. The 10-percenters of all walks of life seem to be quite necessary in many in stances, but to me they have always been a plague both major and minor. I hear jokes about Hollywood agents, but beneath the mirth and ridicule there must be some real truth. Fight managers are licensed individuals, and are thus protected. Fighters who want to fight professionally had better have a manager. I now have two and my manager of record is a man I never talk to, and the man I talk to has been in the game so long I am another can of peas on his grocery shelf waiting to be sold to the highest bidder. Richardson opened my eyes, as Felix and I were friends and partners and Felix was as new to prize fighting as I was. I never considered Felix in a class with the sharpies I have met. Felix didn't know enough, and left the business much too soon to become adroit.

Mickey Richardson had a birthday on board the *Monterey* and we celebrated by throwing his father into the pool. There was water in it. My turn to be tossed in came when the ship crossed the Equator, and as I was a "hardshell" in I went. They knew I couldn't swim so I went into the shallow end, but poor Jack went in again at the deep.

We were traveling cabin or second-class and the fine food three times a day was slowly putting pounds on me. They served tea and cake in the afternoon and I never missed that either. Prior to going to Australia I had no idea of what a diet was and never had trouble making weight or losing it. But now I was eating like a Georgia warden and began to feel uncomfortable around my middle. I now weighed 165 when I should have been 159. I didn't realize it, but I was creating a major problem that later took quite a bit of solving.

I don't want to sound like a snob in reverse but it seemed to me the people in first class didn't have the fun we did. They had to dress for dinner, and an air of formality surrounded their activities. We dressed casually and made friends easily and most of the folks in cabin class were going to Australia to work. Theatrical people, and there were a lot of them, practiced their acts by performing for us at night, and it was like visiting a training camp watching these people sharpen their routines for the main event. I had a ball on that ship, except that I missed Mattie dearly. I wrote to her every day, reporting exactly what happened and telling her of my feelings for her.

There was a popular song not too long ago called *Mixed Emotions*, and I guess that's the best description of my state during the voyage and throughout my stay in Australia. Marriage was a very solemn thing for me, and my involuntary separation seemed to me romantically tragic. But I was going forward to adventure and was bolstered by the thought of what might lie ahead. Little did I know the reverse side of the coin, for marriage and separation had done the opposite for Mattie. She was now cut off socially inasmuch as she was newly married, and the only adventure she could look forward to was her day's work on the job. Evening after evening she spent with her family, with interludes of reading letters telling her what a fine time her groom was having on his solo honeymoon. Absence may make the heart grow fonder, but even a heart can reach a point of no return.

The ship arrived in Honolulu and we went ashore to sight-see and buy the inevitable knickknacks. We visited the pineapple center and were given deluxe treatment, with varieties of pineapple drinks and warm Hawaiian hospitality. When we left they strung flower leis around our necks and the Royal Hawaiian Band played *Aloha*. We were told to throw the leis overboard as we cleared the harbor as it meant we would return. Again a feeling of lonesomeness crept over me as I looked at the islands framed in the sunset while in the wake of the ship the fragile bouquets bobbed on the waves. The shipboard conviviality snapped me out of my mood and as soon as we were 3 miles out gambling was resumed and they held a horse race on deck. I am not now a gambler nor was I then, for nothing dulls the edge of gambling fever as the lack of money.

In two days we reached Samoa, and it was the first time I had ever seen such a mixture of people. You could see boys with gray eyes, dark skin and red hair. Almost any combination of colors. I didn't like Samoa, for it rained every five minutes. A quick shower and then bright sunshine. The native shopkeepers had all the color and innocence of a Delancey Street pawnbroker. We sailed, and the next point we reached was where Amelia Earhart's last message came from, and it was fresh in everyone's mind in 1940 and saddened us all. Two mornings later we arrived at Suva in the Fiji Islands. We had just left the Polynesian people and were now to see the Melanesian race. They were more negroid, with bushy hair. The men wore their hair combed from 9 inches to a foot straight up. If they played football they'd have needed top hats for helmets. They were more interested in seeing me when I got off the ship, as I was another colored man, and being British subjects they spoke English very well. Let's face it, they spoke better than I did. They soon discovered I was a boxer, and to my surprise they were all excited over Joe Louis, who was like a demigod to them. This interest, plus the presence of another American colored fighter, made my arrival a big event. They figured if I was being sent all the way from the States to Australia I must be a very good fighter. I was forced to side with their shrewd figuring.

The other tourists were starting on the usual trek of camera and guide, but these natives insisted I go with them to a village not seen by the ordinary visitor. I was flattered and curious, and away we went.

They had sent a man ahead with instructions to prepare a native feast for me, and I was overwhelmed at their generosity. It was mostly starches, but I ate like a villain's helper as it would have been impolite to make excuses. I could feel the weight gathering around my middle. Then mandolins, tiples and other musical instruments were brought out and the villagers danced and sang for me. I noticed a very curious thing; their music was very close to what I call the music of the "down home" Negro, the Negro who originated jazz. Here on this faraway island you could feel the strains of Dixieland in their primitive melodies. The beat, for instance, was entirely different from the Hawaiian, and it had the same spiritual rhythm you can hear in Mississippi today.

I felt at ease and began to ask a few questions of my own. Not to be too personal, I asked one chap why he had no arms. He replied blithely, "A shark got me." You often wonder how a man is capable of superhuman courage and endurance. A shark had attacked him and snared one arm, and while trying to fight the monster off he lost the other one. Yet he managed to swim away and be rescued. As a prize fighter your courage is measured against your skills, but as a pearl diver your courage covers a bit more distance. Soon I saw many partial amputees and I remarked that sharks were quite dangerous. But they said sharks are actually cowards and that it was a sport of young boys to hunt them armed only with a knife. I wouldn't hunt them with a 10-foot pole.

Back on board the *Monterey* many of the passengers asked where I had been and what had happened. When they heard the natives of Suva Fiji regarded me as a great fighter their own respect increased and I became a popular figure on board ship.

Members of the crew, more avid fight fans than most of the passengers, became my buddies. Later, in Sydney, I often met members of the crew. It's true about sailors; they do have girlfriends in every port. I'd meet them in night clubs and restaurants and it always gave me a warm feeling to enter a place and be greeted by my "shipmates." To a stranger, far from home, these little niceties counted for a lot.

We left Suva, Fiji, and then went to Auckland, New Zealand. Our stops were for loading and unloading cargo, and it gave us all a chance for a visit coupled with the opportunity to add to our trove of souvenirs. I was amazed at the number of nationalities who were in business on the various islands. Chinese, East Indian, Dutch and so on. Their ability to adapt to language and customs of foreign places and make a living was astounding. I don't think Americans can do that as readily, but maybe it is because America is so young. But everywhere, in my travels, I've observed the American expects the foreigner to speak English and seldom makes an effort to learn an alien tongue. We've grown accustomed to speaking with money, and it is a harsh tongue.

The morning after leaving Auckland we arrived in Sydney harbor. We ate a hurried breakfast and prepared to disembark. There was no one waiting. Nobody knew I was there. And nobody knew Jack Richardson. No fanfare for Archie Moore; I was just another fighter shipped to Australia as part of the cargo of the good ship *Monterey*. Finally the secretary from the boxing promoter's office arrived. He introduced himself as Harry Miller, and I'm glad to say that today he's a big boxing promoter himself. Mr. Dick Lean and Mr. Bill Donohue were the big men of boxing at that time. They both had vast interests in Australia—lumber, gold mines—and so boxing was a sideline hobby.

Jack Richardson, being from Memphis, Tennessee, took me to a section of Sydney known as King's Cross and registered me in a hotel. He and Harry Miller got together and found Jack an apartment way across town. So I was left all alone in downtown Sydney in a section like Times Square by a man who was going to guide my destiny. However, I've always been able to adapt to a situation and I've never been afraid of people. I could usually get what I wanted without being humiliated, and in this instance what I wanted was to make good. So my whereabouts just couldn't upset me. Richardson left me, saying he would send someone in the morning who would take me to the gym and that he would meet me there.

Having absolutely nothing to do I went for a walk to see what my new home looked like. Sydney is a big metropolis and as busy as all the others. People and traffic, shops and advertising signs. The city is a cross roads of the Southern Hemisphere, and many nationalities passed by as I strolled and gaped. With the reverse of the seasons it was summer, and the evening was mildly warm. Down the street, coming towards me, I saw a very natty colored boy. Now he wasn't exactly familiar to me, but he did look like he'd been around and it seemed as though I should know him. I'm not in the habit of speaking to strangers just because they're Negroes. Being a member of a minority doesn't mean handshakes and grins. But there was something about this fellow that brought a wide grin of hello to my face, and he smiled cheerily in return. I said "Hi" and he asked me my name. I told him, but it meant nothing to him. But when he said he was Johnny Hutchison I knew his name. He'd fought some of the finest featherweights and lightweights in the East around Philadelphia. He told me that he and Al Brown had been in Australia almost a year. He had just come from a grocery store and invited me for dinner at their apartment, which was just down the block from my hotel. It certainly sounded good to me. I was there promptly at chow time. Johnny had a friend cooking for him, so we sat talking about fighters we had known mutually, and I filled them in on the fight scene in the States. It was truly a memorable evening. My first in Sydney, and it had started out as a miserable lonely night and ended by my making fast friends and having something to do any night I was so inclined. After dinner I insisted they come back to my hotel. When I got there I took out three records I had brought with me. One was Cab Calloway's *Jumpin' Jive* and a Louis Jordan record, *I'm Gonna Move to the Outskirts of Town.* The third was a fine band of 1940, Fletcher Henderson. These records made a big hit with Johnny and Al. They were jitterbugs, and though that particular dance hadn't hit Australia yet, Calloway would be great for dancing in the apartment. We spent many evenings there. Some friends of Johnny's were working Australia then. People like Chuck and Chuckles, a dance team and a singer, Bob Parish. Also, Sunshine Sammy and Sleepy Williams were working the Orpheum Circuit.

So we were quite a group. As fellow Americans we seemed to seek each other's company, and the conversations ranged from fighting to music to show business, so it was never dull. Of course I wrote Mattie of all this, still not realizing how dull her life had become. But as yet I hadn't earned a penny, and would soon be reminded how expensive it was just living down under.

On my first Friday in Sydney, Richardson took me to see my first Australian fight. He also invited Hutchison. Ron Richards, who was a triple-crown champion of Australia, having held the middleweight, light heavyweight and heavyweight titles, was fighting at his best weight, 159 pounds. He had recently beaten Gus Lesnevich, later to become World's Light Heavyweight Champion, and he had a punch that could take the top of your head off. That night he was fighting an Australian contender named Fred Henneberry. Now Australians are great gamblers. They will bet on anything. This fight between two leading Aussies had produced very heavy betting, and after a grueling fight Richards was declared winner in the eleventh round on a foul. A foul voided all bets. Henneberry, not wanting to lose by a knockout or decision, kept fouling Richards, and after two warnings by the referee he fouled him a third time and the fight was awarded to Richards. The crowd, split down the middle, was half furious and half happy. Johnny Hutchison said he had seen this happen often. Evidently an Australian fighter who is losing doesn't want to let down the people who backed him, but it certainly seemed peculiar to me. I think the chap getting fouled had a legitimate beef.

Jack Richardson asked me if I thought I could beat Ron Richards. I considered this and then said I thought I could beat him if I was in the best condition I had ever been in my life. My weight was bothering me, but I didn't say so. I'd been working out every day but the weight I gained on board ship was still with me. Richardson, after much more discussion, finally believed me on my terms and said I'd have to go to the country to train. This was the first time anyone had suggested I go to the country to a training camp. I knew champions and some big name fighters went to camps, but I was used to taking a trolley to go to the gym and running in city parks for my road work.

The match with Richards was made but I caught a virus and had to remain in bed for four or five days, and they changed the match completely. I got a postponement with Richards and was matched with Jack McNamee for a Melbourne fight. I didn't go to a training camp. Instead I went to the city of Melbourne to train where the newspaper writers could get a look at me to help build the gate for the fight. While I was training, Hutchison went on the road. He fought in Adelaide and scored a knockout and then came on to Melbourne where I was. He had seen McNamee fight and advised me to hit him with body smashes, as it would soften him up so I could get to him. It was a good idea to have this fight before the big one with Richards, for if I won "good" it would build interest and make Sydney fans curious to see me in action. The Melbourne press had been kind to me, and when I scored a decisive knock out over McNamee in four rounds I was hailed by the sports writers. McNamee told me it was like having hot steel poured on his ribs. This quote appeared in both Melbourne and Sydney and drummed up interest in me as a visiting fighter.

At that time, just prior to the McNamee fight, Richardson had found a trainer for me. He was an old-time Aussie fighter, and the thing I remember most about Ike Kutner was his total disregard for money. He cared nothing at all about it. All that concerned Ike was having a winner and having that winner in the best possible shape. Ike was a better conditioner than he was a teacher. I didn't really need a boxing coach. I realize that in the length of time it takes you to read this far you may think I'm a little cocky about my skill, but

I had had many, many fights and my "shell" style was developed and my science was now my own. But Ike was a body builder deluxe. It's not quite enough for a trainer to understand exercise and boxing; he must be able to talk to a fighter and build his confidence and keep his spirits up. Ike, Hiawatha Grey and Dick Saddler have always been able to do this for me.

To get ready for the Ron Richards fight Richardson sent me to a ranch in the Megalong Valley. It is about 70 miles outside Sydney. It was my first contact with the aborigines, who, before the advent of the English settlers, lived in perfect harmony with their gods and with nature. When I first told a reporter I had learned the secrets of weight control from these natives he gave me the tongue-in-cheek routine you so often get when you try to tell the truth. If I had informed him I made the weight by slicing strips from my backside with a straight razor he'd probably have come closer to believing me. But since the writer wanted a story, and since space in the papers selfishly means there will be more in it for Moore, I embellished the yarn a bit and told him the aborigine admired a heavy red sweater I was wearing and wanted to trade for it. He whispered the secret diet in my ear and I gave him the sweater in return for the diet and his boomerang, which I haven't been able to throw away since.

First let me explain my problem. I was not overweight in the lay sense of the word. Every ounce on my body was solid, hardened flesh. I was overweight for fighting, but the very solidness was the big problem. Normally, a person beginning to diet sheds the first pounds quickly, since much of it is bloat, or weight caused by liquids. I was over 160 by a few pounds, but 160 was the weight limit for middleweights and if I couldn't get below it meant I'd have to fight as a light heavyweight and give away almost 15 pounds. I'd be fighting men who weighed 170 to 175 pounds and, frankly, at that time, I didn't want to. I later developed into a light heavyweight and really am now considered a heavyweight, but in Australia I was a kid and wanted to fight Richards at his prime weight of 159.

What little experience I had had in making weights was bad. As an amateur back in St. Louis I wanted to fight a welterweight, named Billy Sims, and I weighed 150 which was 3 pounds over the welter limit of 147. So I set about to lose the 3 pounds. I sought a professional to whom I attributed the wisdom of Solomon and asked him how to lose weight.

"It's a cinch," he said. "All you have to do is take Epsom salts. You'll lose all the weight you want."

Armed with this worthy counsel, I began taking salts and continued for ten days. It took off the weight, but it didn't stop there. When I weighed in for Sims I was 139. I'd taken off 11 pounds and none of it was fat. I thought the old pro was a genius.

In the first round I pounded Sims all over the ring. I had him ready to go, but the bell saved him. The bell that spared him nearly killed me. When I got back to my corner, my legs gave out and I hit the stool hard. It wasn't what had just happened but what was going to happen. I could hardly get to my feet for the second round and I don't know how I got through it. They awarded Sims the decision in the third round because I was too weak to throw a punch, much less get out of the way of one.

This memory haunted me in the Megalong Valley. I boarded with a family named Baptiste. They treated me like a son and a brother. I'll never forget them. The mother is dead now, and I would have liked to have seen her once again before she died. One of the girls, Georgina, who was nine years old then, is now an accomplished concert pianist in London. Another daughter, Norma, married an American army officer and now lives in Cleveland. I visited them later, in 1947, when I boxed Ezzard Charles. Then there was Bella and Lee, and Joe, Jules and Johnny, whom I still write to. They made my stay a wonderful one and they put up with the system I devised for losing weight.

For the first time in my life I had the perfect place to train. I did my roadwork in the pleasant valley, making a lot of friends and learning much about Australian history and customs. The Black Heath Mountains, which bordered the valley, were a backdrop that would enhance any movie screen. I came in contact with the aborigines and they were friendly to me, and as I got to know them better I noticed I never saw a fat aborigine. These people had the reputation of possessing incredible endurance. I heard stories of how they were capable of crossing hundreds of miles in the desolate Australian bush country with only a pouch of dried meat. It dawned on me they must derive their staying power from their diet or living habits, and probably both.

On those fantastically long treks through the wilderness, they got by on the strength they received by chewing the dried meat. The essence of the meat was their secret. They swallowed no bulk but chewed and chewed on a piece of jerked beef until every last drop of juice was extracted, and then chewed some more. As for water, they were known to go days without it. They were noted for finding "soaks" (rock depressions holding rain water), and for locating plants containing water and chewing leaves pulled from them. I'd even heard of this ancient race hunting frogs to kill them later on for the water they contained.

To me there was a pattern. These Stone Age people, who were so beautifully adapted to their environment before civilization disrupted it, got their strength from the natural juices of the plants and animals they ate. They got by on a fraction of the food consumed by their more civilized brothers. But they seemed to be better men physically as a consequence.

The solution to my problem was in sight. If they got by on the juices of what they ate, so could I. If it was possible for me to keep my strength just with the liquid that entered my body from chewing my food, why did I have to swallow the bulk? I tried it. I chewed each delicious piece of medium rare steak until there was not a drop of moisture left and then discarded what was left. Of course I ate alone, and the Baptiste family understood what I was trying to do.

After a week I found I was as strong as ever and had lost two pounds. Two pounds of too, too solid flesh.

To insure my reduction plan I limited myself to a pint of water a day, putting the pint bottle in the refrigerator so I could pace my drinking by noting the contents of the bottle. To further augment the diet, I drank the broth of cooked vegetables and did not eat the bulk. My weight problem was licked and all that remained was to find, through trial and error, which foods and vegetables were best suited for this kind of experiment. The results are printed in the back of this book.

May I point out that chewing without swallowing is not easy? It is agony, and it will nearly drive you crazy not to swallow a succulent cut of meat. And at first I was a constant back-slider, gulping down an occasional morsel, but my will to lose weight was stronger than my tastebuds, and now I can use this method with no qualms. A diet like this will result in the shrinking of the stomach, which will limit your appetite even after you have finished with the diet. Control liquid intake. Soft drinks and coffee breaks are out. Nowadays in training I take multiple vitamins to supplement my diet. Vitamins are in no way unnatural, and are vital to the attainment of health. They are available to us in food and sunshine, but often vitamins are lost through cooking and it's a rare man who obtains all the sunshine he needs. My old friends, the aborigines, wear little or no clothing and sleep outdoors. The amount of vitamin D they soak up greatly contributes to their resistance, ruggedness and over-all good health.

People dieting should stay away from alcohol. I am not a heavy drinker. I may occasionally have a cold glass of beer on a hot day and once in a while some wine with a meal. I have made it a rule not even to have that little in public, for it would soon be exaggerated into a four-day bender. But alcohol in itself is a double problem to a person who wants to lose weight. It is liquid and it has calories. One glass of beer has a hundred calories. Look up the calorie count on hard liquor. That's the answer.

At the end of my stay in the Megalong Valley I was in the pink of condition and felt better than I ever have in my life. I would have absolutely no alibi if I lost the fight to Ron Richards. As it turned out I almost did have an alibi, and one that would never have stood up with the fans.

I returned to Sydney, minus my red sweater and clutching my boomerang, and found the newspapers had been beating the drum over the forthcoming fight. The excitement before a fight always presages the number of people who will attend. This excitement was like Toots Shor's old bar the night before a big title fight in New York. The papers were trying to develop a feud between Richards and me. They made up quotes saying what I had said about him and what he had said about me. I took it in good fun and hope he did. But a grudge fight is well attended, and we both wanted that. No TV then.

I had been writing Mattie steadily but her answers came sporadically. I believe she was busy, and thought nothing of it. Had I read the letters more closely, read between the lines, I would have detected a bitterness that was developing. I had made some money, true, but this fight with Richards was to be the big payday in Australia, and I still believed I could send for Mattie if I won, and move around Australia fighting all comers. However, I'd read her letters sort of innocently and then go on about my business, which was fighting.

The fight was to be held in Rushcutter's Bay, and I believe that was where Jack Johnson knocked out Tommy Burns to win the heavyweight title. We rented a Bentley automobile to take us out to the arena. It seated about 15,000 people, and there was standing room only that night. My trainer Ike Kutner, decided we would stay home until the last possible minute, and he would wrap my hands at home. He wrapped them too tight, but at the moment I didn't notice it. I was young and eager and thinking of too many other things. My "American group" had assembled to wish me luck and there was a festive air and a carnival spirit, so my hand bandages meant nothing to me then.

I got in the ring and stared at the biggest crowd I had ever seen turn out to see Archie Moore fight. Helen Hayes and I have one thing in common: we both like to look out and see those people. Richards was introduced first, and he bowed in all four directions, which, I learned later, is an old Australian custom. When I was introduced I only bowed once, but the crowd accepted this from an American. I guess I had some backers in that crowd who had wagered a few bob or so. I was beginning to feel the bandages as I waited for the bell. Bandaging a fighter's hands is for protection against breaking small bones, but when they are wrapped too tight they can impair the circulation and numbness sets in, which is dangerous. Without feeling in the hand, you might loosen the clench of your fist and smash knuckles and fingers against an opponent's head.

Kutner gave me a last warning about Richards' terrible punch and the bell rang and out I went. We met in mid-ring and I jabbed once and it fell short and he countered with a right. I can almost feel that punch right now. I was down and could taste blood on the inside of my mouth. I could hear the crowd booing and yelling. Cries of "Fake!" resounded in the air above me. I got up at the count of nine. I shifted from my usual shell defense to a crab defense. Face covered, one eye peeping under a thumb and forearms and elbows taking all the punches. I clinched whenever I saw an opportunity. I wasn't fighting at this point; I was trying to stay alive. I was concentrating on making my head clear, but that's difficult when you're getting bone-crushing, jarring punches every second or so. Slowly I came out of it and began to box him very carefully, highly defensively. I found Richards wanting in this respect as he was basically a savage puncher and not a boxer. I forced him to box, as punchers need to get set solidly to really throw their "Sunday" punch. I kept moving, moving, never letting him get set and never keeping myself stationary either. In the third round I managed to nuisance-jab so much I got his nose bleeding. In the fourth I moved up with my jabs and cut him over both eyes. The fifth and sixth rounds found me worrying these wounds, and in the seventh he made a tremendous rally but I was able to hold him in check. During the eighth I managed to open a few more cuts on his lips and ear and he looked a mess. I was covered with his blood and didn't look too much better. The ninth round started, and it was obvious to me that Richards was as through as he would ever be. I was disgusted at the amount of punishment they were letting him take but let his cousins worry; this was just business to me, though a grim one at that moment. In the tenth round they stopped the fight. He was as game a fighter as I have ever fought, and the amount of punishment he took would have worn well on Hitler.

The next morning I was in sports headlines all over Australia. You recall my saying Richards was a triple crown holder, so beating him in those days was like beating Joe Louis in the States. In just two fights in Australia I had become a "name" fighter. My victory had enough importance to give me a rating internationally among middleweights as a result. Richards, who had beaten Lesnevich, had a reputation in the United States which I now inherited.

I had five more fights in Australia, one of which took me to Tasmania, where I beat Frank Lindsay. I fought Henneberry again and won by a K.O. in seven. I fought Richards again and won in twelve rounds. I visited Adelaide, Australia, and beat Joe Delaney. This is not in chronological order, but all of my fights in Australia were victories. I think Hobart, Tasmania, is as far from Jacobs' Beach as a fighter can possibly get. In my return match with Richards I didn't knock him out, because I broke my hand in the second round. My left hand, my jabbing hand and the one I used against punchers. The hand that keeps them moving. But I did fool him about my injury, and won the decision.

Breaking my hand meant it was time to leave Australia. And to me it meant no one would ever wrap my hand again. I do it for myself, and if anything goes wrong I have myself to blame. I had been in Australia for eight months—January to September. Mattie was waiting. I had been writing, but each time I wrote the possibility of her joining me got dimmer and dimmer. Expenses, the man kept saying, expenses. I had been sending her money all along but in truth it couldn't have been too much, since expenses were deducted before I got money and I had to live, too. I had been saving as much as I could, as I had it in mind to buy a little place of our own. I am a firm believer in owning a place to live. No matter what misfortune overtakes you, you have a place to stay, a roof over your head. When I finally did get home I had $800 saved. It figures to a hundred a month profit for five tough fights in Australia and a broken hand. But don't get me wrong; I love the fight game.

As a nice coincidence I was booked on the *Monterey* for the return voyage, and this time everybody on board hailed me. They had been reading about me on the front pages and many had seen me fight. But the trip was made when Great Britain was at war. We Americans had three months or so to wait before Pearl Harbor. A Canadian ship had been sunk right outside the harbor. The United States had ordered all citizens to return home. Due to the submarine menace, the ship was routed off its usual course and we went from New Zealand to Tahiti. The girls were very beautiful and wore sarongs and flowers in their hair. When we arrived the *Mariposa*, a ship going in the other direction, had already arrived, and having two big ships at one time made it a festive occasion for the Tahitians, and we were swept along by their enthusiastic welcomes. The French franc had already started to drop, and the sight of American dollars caused the Tahitians to give rousing cheers. When I got off the ship the franc was forty to the dollar and I bought about $25 worth of perfume for Mattie. Unfortunately the bottle broke in my trunk and the trunk had an irresistible scent for two years. Then the black market took over the money exchange, and as we were there for three days the fun was on. On board ship were four Filipinos trying to get back to Manila. One was called Fighting Carlos. Fighting Carlos had been fighting dice since the day we left Sydney and he had dropped about $400. A man approached me about staging a fight, since night life in Tahiti wasn't exactly like New Orleans. We had the people, they had the money, so why not supply fighters and make a gentle exchange? I had a broken hand, but still thought the idea was sound and I knew

I could locate Fighting Carlos. I told the man to dig up a local contender and I would supply the Filipino champ who was traveling incognito as Fighting Carlos. Carlos hadn't had a fight in a month, but stooping to pick up the dice had kept him limber and I knew he had to recoup his gambling losses. I had arranged for him to get a $250 guarantee. I went to Carlos' cabin and found him in a wine stupor. I shook him awake and asked him how long it would take him to get into shape. I meant wake up. He asked when the fight was. I said in a few hours. He then asked who was going to fight him and I told him a local boy and he grinned and said he'd be ready. As I left, Fighting Carlos returned to pounding the pillow for his training exercises.

When I returned to fetch Carlos shortly before fight time I discovered the prospect of making $250 had called for a small celebration, and he and his buddies had had a few more nips of wine. I finally stuck him under the cold shower, rubbed ice on his face, chest and neck and got him into his fighting togs. His pals helped by singing Philippine marching songs and slapping me on the back. By the time we got to the ring he was walking by himself, but that was about all. Before I could get down from the ring apron at the first bell, the local boy was all over Carlos like a duck on a June bug and was pounding him like a vineyard worker in his own corner. All Carlos did was put up his hands to cover his face and slowly sink to the canvas. He refused to fight. The shrewd promoter, sensing a spot of trouble, cut the round a mite bit short and rang the bell after these thirty seconds of mayhem. I tried to get Fighting Carlos to go out for the second round but as far as he was concerned the next round was on the house, not on him. The crowd booed, and in all fairness to Carlos I must say he didn't mind it too much. The local boy was declared the winner but the booing was pretty strong and I had a heckuva time trying to collect Carlos' purse. I had a broken hand so I threatened the man with legal action. I finally got him his money. But Fighting Carlos was a fiend for wine and slot machines and he blew the $250 before we reached Honolulu. He had a ticket from Hawaii to Manila so I knew he would get home—barely.

On my return to the States I was met by my wife, and Jack Richardson, who had left Australia before I did. What with war rumbles and an ever-growing submarine menace, he had wanted to get his wife and child home safe, and he took the first passage he could get and did so with my sincere blessing.

Almost immediately I sensed a subconscious resentment in Mattie. My stories about my "adventures" and my recounting of the fights I had had seemed to mean nothing to her. There was no communication. Literally, we were strangers. The long separation had counted ten over our marriage. Our marriage was on the rocks, but I did get a little house and try. It was the first house I ever owned, but even there Richardson got in the deal and held my notes, and the complications mounted until I lost both house and wife. Mattie is dead now, but she was my first love and I always thought she should have had a better chance than what fate dealt her.

# ROUND 6 KNIGHT IN ARMOR

My auntie was living in San Diego with us. After my wife left me I lost my home, and I resumed my friendly relationship with Linn Platner and began to fight again, a favorite son of San Diego, the man who had beaten the Australian champion. I was a big frog in a small pond. But as small ponds go, this one was the best. I knew now that San Diego would always be my home, and I made plans to start a business of some sort. Not that I contemplated retiring from the ring, but I needed a business that could earn me money while I was between fights or in training. I wasn't much of a businessman but I knew what I liked. I liked fried chicken.

Fried chicken has a personality all its own. It's traditionally been considered a Southern specialty, but like the Schmoo it has many purposes. It can be a full meal or a between-meal snack. It can be eaten at a table or while riding in a car. If you can't finish what you've got, wrap it in a napkin and it will keep for some time. You can eat it hot or cold with fork or freehand-style. You can fry a chicken a bit at a time or all at once, depending on your volume of trade. And best of all, chicken is cheap and anyone can learn to fry it. So, armed with these statistics after a lifetime of research and wiping my chin, I decided to open a chicken shack and began putting money aside for that purpose. But something happened that forced me to delay donning a chef's hat and greasing up my pan.

I had won three fights and lost two since my return from Australia. Shorty Hogue had beaten me twice. A professional fighter expects a loss now and then, so I wasn't too upset about Hogue. He was good, and it was no disgrace to lose to him. My popularity had not diminished and I was matched against Eddie Booker, a ranking fighter, on February 26, 1941. Looking back, I realize that worry over my marital state had affected me more than I knew. When I went into the ring against Booker I was in a good state of mind but, unbeknownst to me, my physical condition was poorer than it had ever been. I fought Booker and it was a tough fight. It went the full ten rounds and was declared a draw. I dressed and went home, another day's work done.

The next afternoon I was raking leaves in the warm sun waiting for my date, Catherine Turner, to arrive, as we were going for a drive up the coast. I had been seeing Catherine quite steadily for some time, but since my first marriage had been such a disaster I was not too eager to think about divorce and remarriage. Catherine understood this and had never pressed the issue, so my life was serene, the sun was warm and I worked pleasantly. Suddenly, as though a knife had been thrown swiftly into my stomach, I doubled over in pain. Sharp, agonizing darts of pain in my abdomen. I had already dropped the rake and stood swaying, clutching my stomach with both hands and trying to remember if Booker had hit me there during the fight the night before. Idiotically, I thought this was a delayed pain from a punch. I tumbled over as my auntie, who had been on the back porch, came running to me. The next thing I remember was being driven to the hospital.

The hospital was very crowded, and it seemed to take forever to get a doctor to examine me. I was finally admitted to the examining room but they now began to ask questions and wanted my life history. I thought it was a horrible waste of time as the pain made it almost impossible to concentrate on what they were saying, but Auntie answered for me as I writhed in a chair while Catherine tried to comfort me.

A young doctor, John Pollack, was assigned to me, and I was suffering such intense pain he had to force me to lie flat. He asked me to relax my stomach muscles. I couldn't. They began to tap and probe, took my temperature, blood count, et cetera, and it seemed to go on for ages. Tears and sweat trickled over my face. Dr. Pollack said I had a perforated ulcer, and would have to have an immediate operation. With all the pain, I almost flipped lying there, for I felt abdominal surgery would be the end of Archie Moore, fighter. But X-ray and fluoroscope confirmed his diagnosis. So it seemed the ring record book would snap shut: Moore fought from 1936 to 1940, Amen.

Back in some corner of my mind a memory fought to get out. I recalled meeting a fighter who had resumed boxing after an operation for appendicitis. And he had told me he had asked the doctor to make the incision a certain way—to cut along the muscles and separate them rather than cut through. I pleaded with my doctor almost incoherently to make a similar incision, but he did understand and he did perform the operation just that way, and I still thank him fervently for doing just that. Many people seated at ringside have noticed the scar shaped like a hockey stick on my stomach, and it is the result of Dr. Pollack making the incision down the solar plexus and then sideways.

I was given a spinal anesthetic and was allowed to watch the operation in an overhead mirror. Being numb from the neck down, it was as though I was watching a picture or seeing a total stranger under the knife. After a while I did become nauseous and the spinal effect seemed to be wearing off and I grew very warm. I glanced over at the bellows that indicated my breathing rate and it was quivering. I thought to myself, This is it, and began repeating over and over, I've got to live, I've got to live. Then I passed out.

Prayer was no stranger to me. My auntie had given me a good religious foundation and it seemed natural now to pray for my life. Not that I was too young to die; many boys my age and younger were dying in battle at that moment, but I was asking God to spare me for my auntie. She had been so wonderful to us all and had devoted her life to raising us and now it seemed there would be no one to protect her. I thought if God took me He would surely be taking her, too. The phrase I've got to live, I've got to live droned on and on in my semiconscious mind the clock around. I was in a room with two beds, and a fellow in the other bed aroused me by calling my name.

"Archie, Archie. Are you awake?" I slowly opened my eyes and the room swirled into focus. I looked at him blankly.

"You've been mumbling for hours, Archie." He looked at me quizzically. "Say, don't you remember me?" I weakly shook my head. "I was at your house last week. I'm Johnny Brown."

I smiled wanly, but I didn't remember him. It took a week for me to recognize him. We used to call him Johnny Mack Brown after a famous movie star of the time. I never did recall his visit to the house, although my auntie remembered it clearly. Johnny had had a terrible accident. He was a construction worker and had fallen from a scaffold. As he said, he stepped back to admire his work.

I now discovered I had been unconscious for five days, and learned that a young friend of mine, Junior Elras Salvador, had donated a pint of his blood for the transfusion that I so badly needed and that stimulated my recovery. Needless to say, Junior and I are still great friends today.

I was a captive audience of my mind. I had nothing to do but think. Most of my thinking up to now had to do with boxing and boxing strategy. But I was beginning to take stock of myself as an individual. I was a man with a direction in life, but no purpose. My chicken shack would be one purpose, and the recovery and retention of my health would be the other. I was trying to determine how a man who lived a clean, athletic life could come down with such a severe case of ulcers. I always believed ulcers came from drinking. But I later found out that worry or extreme tension is the major cause. I was in the hospital for thirty-eight days. I weighed 163 pounds when I entered the hospital, and was discharged weighing 108.

Mr. Platner, the San Diego fight promoter, was very nice to me. He sent a specialist to examine me, and the reassurance of this expert did much to calm my fears. Dr. Pollack had indeed done a fine job.

Outside my window was a beautiful eucalyptus tree, and in the early hours of the morning I could detect the first traces of sunlight glistening on the leaves about thirty minutes before the sun rose. And as this tree, a reminder of Australia, got tinted red I would reach for the Bible and read the book of Gideon. The sunlight became an obsession. I longed to sit in the sun; the desire was over powering. No man can fully appreciate how fortunate he is until he is totally helpless and can no longer do the things he used to take for granted. That old saying, the best things in life are free, must have a lot of truth in it, for all I wanted was the sunshine and I knew it would do me a world of good. I convinced myself of this and implored the doctor to let me have just fifteen minutes of sunshine, but each day he would stall me by saying maybe tomorrow.

I now found out I had survived peritonitis. At that time it was fatal in a great number of cases, since drugs like penicillin were not in common use, if at all. I think I beat peritonitis by having a body that was extremely fit. Following peritonitis I developed pneumonia, a common after-effect. Although I didn't have my chicken shack yet, it was definitely a case of out of the frying pan into the fire. I was facing an uphill struggle, but at least I had the chance to struggle, which is more than I had bargained for. I was grimly determined to master my mind and strike worry and apprehension from my everyday thoughts.

Years later, in the late fall of 1955, I was sitting on the lawn in front of my training quarters at North Adams, Massachusetts, with a group of sports writers. It was a couple of weeks before I was to fight Rocky Marciano for the World's Heavyweight Championship. The boys and I were having an informal press conference.

We had already covered the usual stuff about my weight, how I felt, what my battle plan would be, and so on, and the questions had begun to fall off. It was a drowsy, warm afternoon in the Berkshires and I had almost dozed off when one reporter casually asked me how old I was. I replied as I always did, but I could see he didn't believe me. Why, I don't know. Then he asked about my "secret" diet. This has always been a fun subject to reporters, and I had explored the subject about as much as I could. I even had a lock put on the training camp refrigerator, pretending my secrets were too valuable to be left lying around. I used to carry a flask filled with bouillon and sip from it, saying it was brewed by a tribe of aborigines who had adopted me. When I ate meals I had a screen put up around my table. That part was all fun. But now I decided to tell this reporter one true facet of my diet and see how he would take it. The thing I decided to tell him was evolved lying on that hospital bed in San Diego in 1940.

I told him one of the main ingredients of my diet and my longevity in the ring was "relaxism." All the reporters laughed at this. There was no such word, but they thought I had used the word out of ignorance and I let it go at that. Two favorite words of mine are "relaxism" and "escapism." I think both of them fit what I mean. They filed funny stories—publicity!

In the hospital, I reasoned to myself that bitterness is very impractical for people in general and for athletes in particular. To be healthy a man must master the art of relaxism, and a bitter man cannot do it. My race, down through history, has had cause for bitterness. But so many of us found the futility of giving way to this character-rotting, health-wrecking emotion. During the years of slavery and the years of economic exploitation that followed and still exists in some part, the Negro developed an escapist outlook. If nothing could be done about the situation, then why not go along with the way the wind blew?

Fortunately there were a lot of colored men who couldn't accept that way of life. The great colored fighting men down through the years were among this group. Nobody gets into a ring to fight unless he believes in his manhood. A lot of those old-timers kept their mental balance by fighting, by working off the steam of frustration on an opponent.

Now that education among colored people is becoming more and more widespread, I've read that the incidence of mental illness has also surged upward among them. That's easy for me to understand. Now that they can't respect the backward philosophy of their elders, they become filled to the breaking point with bitterness, and the tension generated by this useless, harmful emotion is bound to wreck their health mentally and physically.

Frustration is not restricted to colored people. Many people of all races are eaten up with hate for their employers, their jobs, their competitors, their mates. I came to know a great deal about the evil emotions of the human spirit because I was obsessed with so many of them. And because of these feelings I was now lying in a bed recuperating from surgery.

I was eaten with ambition and bitter because I never seemed to get my due as a fighter. I knew just how good I was, and that wasn't vanity. But in the hospital I weighed my assets. The main asset was that I was still alive and I knew I would fight again, although the doctor had told my auntie I should forget it. I got rid of my bitterness lying there, and in the years to come it is a good thing I did so, for the long campaign to get a shot at the light heavyweight title was the most frustrating thing that ever could have happened to me.

I began to make an effort to relax. Now this sounds odd, but I devised little systems to completely relax my body by doing so a toe at a time, a leg at a time, and so on until the last finger lay on the bedspread in blissful contentment. I got better and better at it, and today I can grab five minutes of refreshing sleep in a room full of people.

The main secret of true relaxism, friends, is diversion. It is easy to tell someone to leave his work in the office when he quits for the day, but not so easy to practice. You have to have some diversion. I always loved music and after leaving the hospital I started collecting jazz. Today I have thousands of hours of wonderful music recorded on tapes, and I play them constantly. Any hobby will serve the purpose. Stamp collecting, bird watching or dirigible photography are all diversions that take a man's mind off his problems. A person who has no hobby has no life. Poker, bowling or kite flying, they are all brothers in a family that will help you relax if you invite them over.

Now that my mental attitude seemed to be well adjusted, I concentrated on getting well. I still wanted sunshine, and there didn't seem to be any way to get it. I rebelled against the food and made myself a general nuisance. (This was a nice diversion.) One night I had a setback that sent my fever up and the nurses thought I wouldn't last the night. But I was there when my auntie arrived on schedule, as she always did, and gave me the ice cream she made for me. She made it for me every night. That morning she carried along a jar of chicken broth, and the nurse came in just as I was swallowing this delicious nectar. Instead of stopping me she said I could eat anything I wanted to if I wanted to kill myself. I was so fed up with the hospital diet, strained foods prepared in the blandest fashion, that I took the nurse up on that kind offer. I tasted the last of the chicken broth and asked my auntie to bring me some fried chicken. Catherine brought the chicken over later in the day with some crackers and more broth. I hid this treasure under my pillow and after I was served my daily ration of jello I reached under the pillow and ate the champion piece of chicken of all time. But by now the doctor and the nurses thought I was a hopeless case and they let me have my own way. I ate and ate, and Auntie's cooking got me stronger and stronger.

I was supposed to be ready to leave on the thirty-fifth day, but midnight came and I was awake and anxious for the sun to rise and I pulled out the tube that ran from my nose into my stomach. I was in the middle of doing this when the nurse came and counter-punched me pushing the tube right back. For my bit of self-reliance the referee in white penalized me two more days. Finally, on the morning of the thirty-eighth day, I was ready to leave. Coming into the hospital, I had made myself a promise that I would walk out just as I had walked in. I asked my auntie to bring a mirror with her that morning, because I wanted to see myself; I had no mirror in my room. I was truly horrified! I had no neck, my cheeks were shrunken, and I had some old man's face. Long, long hair, and I thought I was looking at Dorian Gray at the end of the trail. My aunt had brought my smallest suit and my smallest shirt. I could slip the shirt on without unbuttoning the collar and the suit hung on me like a landlord's agent. I was able to stroll around in my shoes and had to stuff paper in them to keep them from falling off. I was surprised that my fingernails fit. Just then the nurse came in wheeling a wheelchair. I refused to sit in it; I wanted to walk out. I leaned my shoulder against the wall and scraped my way to the elevator, and when it arrived I clung to the rail. My aunt and nurse held my arms and I walked outside to Catherine's car. They opened the door, and I asked Catherine to move, and I slid behind the wheel and drove the car home.

Vanity had given me the strength to drive home, and doing so made me feel better than I actually was. After I'd been home a few hours, my aunt said she had to go for the laundry but I insisted I could go get it. The laundry was only two blocks away and it was downhill. I forgot I would be walking uphill coming back. I made it to the laundry all right but just couldn't get back up. I was able to wave a car to stop, and the boy in it didn't recognize me at first, I had changed so much. But when he did he gladly drove me home. I went right to bed and slept the clock around. Now that I was home I began to eat in earnest, although I stuck to the antacid diet the doctors had prescribed.

Catherine Turner knew it would be a long time before I'd be able to work, so she took over the support of my aunt, niece and myself. What money I had saved had long since gone for my extensive medical bills. Catherine insisted I was to think of nothing but getting well, as we both knew the dangers of worry after an ulcer operation.

I tried, but each day I would spend more time thinking of what I had to do and how soon I could do it. I had to get a job, for boxing was out of the question for a year or maybe more. Women like Catherine Turner are few and far between, and I count myself lucky to have met her. So I sat at home, or went walking on the beach when Catherine had time to drive me there, and I thought and thought about the financial predicament I was in. It was hard to practice my new theory of relaxism; the ever-present problems of day-to-day living were all too apparent to me. I was getting more than embarrassed about accepting Catherine's good works. My weight had gone up from 108 to 120, but I couldn't seem to gain any more than that. Slowly, ounce by ounce, I gained another 15 pounds, but then my weight stayed exactly at 135. It was most puzzling: I was eating and resting but not gaining weight.

One day we were returning from the beach and I was drowsily sitting in the car as Catherine drove when I got a severe pain in the abdomen. I doubled over, clutching my stomach, and Catherine stopped the car. I told her this was exactly what had happened the first time, and I didn't believe I'd be able to pull through if it meant undergoing another operation. I wondered if the doctor had made some sort of error that was just coming to the surface now. Catherine tried to reassure me by saying it couldn't possibly be ulcers again, but I was positive and I was ready to give up completely. The pain didn't subside, and Catherine drove me directly to the hospital.

This time I was admitted without delay and the doctor quickly diagnosed my condition as acute appendicitis. I screamed and yelled. Why hadn't they removed the appendix when I was cut open the first time? They explained they hadn't taken out my heart and lungs either; there wasn't any reason to. Now I was told I had to be operated on immediately and I was assured this operation was not as complicated as the previous one and I would be up and walking around in a matter of days. I was dubious, but they were right. I was up and around in a week. This time I let Catherine drive me home. No heroics.

Very shortly after that I gained weight rapidly, and in no time at all I was up to 155. It was now imperative that I find a job. San Diego, being a big naval and marine base, was a beehive of activity at this time. Housing was needed for the thousands of war workers who flocked to the area. A big project was being built in dormitory fashion and maintenance men were required to keep the grounds and buildings in order. The man I was told to see was a former athlete, Milton Kraft, one-time fly-casting champion. He's now in the sporting goods business and still a good friend of mine.

I went to see Mr. Kraft. He was an exact double for one of my old heroes in the movies, Jack Holt. Since he had followed my ring career he was more interested in talking about that than about a job for me. I answered in grunts, impatient to know if I was going to work or not. My last grunt turned to a grin when he assured me he had a job for me, but first let's talk about Australian fighters.

I had asked him for maintenance work, but he said it mostly consisted of pushing lawn mowers and doing handy-man work that would be too strenuous for me at this time. He was going to make me a night watchman at a trailer court that housed navy personnel. All I had to do was make the rounds three times a night, and he gave me a trailer to take a nap in. I made my first round when I came on duty, the next at 11 p.m. and the last at 3 a.m. I was on that job for two months and each day I grew stronger. When I came to work I hobbled more than walked and had a doubled-over posture. Mr. Kraft said when he first saw me he thought I was an old man stirred by patriotism looking for a job. To pass the time at night I started mild exercise and soon had my posture corrected and my walking improved to the point where I could dog trot around the trailer camp. One night Mr. Kraft came to investigate, because some tenants had reported someone moving around behind the trailers. He surprised me at my midnight "roadwork" and was so impressed by the change in my physical being that he decided to give me a better job. I acquired a manually operated lawn mower and must have cut acres and acres of grass. It was a double benefit, because I got more money and the exercise was just what I needed. The lawn mower was light and the ground fairly flat, so the work wasn't too tiring to a convalescent.

One day my old sidekick Felix Thurman came by the house. He thought he had an idea how both of us could make some money. You can't hate a man for ideas like that. He had devised armor for me to wear in the ring. He took a heavy rubber foul cup, the customary support worn in the ring, with a high waist band, and with a razor he split it in the center. Inside the split he inserted an automobile license plate. Then with a soldering iron he sealed the rubber. I now had a metal guard to protect my incision, and I could fight again. To this day I have no idea if this is illegal, but I grabbed at it in desperation. I knew that if I returned to the ring anyone matched against me would be shooting for my stomach, since my operations were known of in the fight world. I trained hard on a right hand to pick off left hooks to the body. I went to work in earnest. I kept the job but began serious roadwork in the early morning, and when my day of grass-trimming was over I went directly to the gym to punch the bag, skip rope and box with anyone who felt like it. I had to let myself be hit on my armor-plating to build my confidence in this protective shield. Once in the ring, in a professional fight, I would have enough to think about without pampering my stomach. The shield worked fine. No one detected it, and eleven months and two days after my operation I put on my armor and fought Bobby Britt of Phoenix and won by a knockout in three rounds. I followed that with four more knockouts in a row, including such tough customers as Shorty Hogue and Tabby Romero. But sports writers were still skeptical about my stamina and general durability after undergoing surgery and returning to fight in less than a year. They all felt I had been lucky and had not yet been hit where it would harm me. They felt that if a fighter did get a solid shot at my stomach that one punch would finish me. To settle the matter once and for all Mr. Platner arranged for a match with Jack Chase. The hooting began for real, for Chase had won his last twenty-two fights. We were in the same weight division. All the papers seemed to accept the fact that I couldn't possibly win, and the only speculations that were made were based on how many rounds I would last. Five K.O.'s in a row meant nothing to them, so I knew I would have to prove I could stay the limit against a top-notch fighter. I planned the fight as much for my own satisfaction as I did to prove to them that I was all right.

I tagged Chase with a vicious left hook and decked him in the second round. I could have swarmed in and finished him but I purposely held back. I wanted to prove to myself that I could go the limit. I had hurt his eye rather badly, and now concentrated on not hitting it, because if I wanted to stay ten rounds he'd have to stay with me. I won seven of ten rounds and felt I had outboxed him to everyone's satisfaction. I won the fight and my self-confidence. I knew now I was ready for the big time.

Jack Richardson was still my manager of record, as he held my contract, but Felix Thurman had devised the plan that made it possible for me to fight again. I felt I owed it to Felix to clarify my managerial situation, and so I appeared before the State Boxing Commission in Los Angeles, and they asked Richardson to appear and show cause as to why he should remain as my manager. The commission ruled in my favor, and Richardson agreed to take a fair price for my contract, which they would set. They learned he had paid $250 for the contract when he bought it and, so they set a price of $450 for my release. He accepted it, and it was one of the best bargains since the Indians sold Manhattan Island.

But things didn't quite jell with Felix. He was a good man but somehow our views didn't jibe. He liked to make things complicated, and I liked to do things direct. After all, fighting is sort of a direct business. I decided to go on my own, and for the first time I was a semi-free agent. The "semi" was, where do I get $450?

Mr. Platner had it. But Platner, according to regulations, couldn't manage a fighter because he was a promoter. So he drew up a contract between his brother and myself. He had acquired virtual control of his hottest attraction, and that was all right with me, for it was to my advantage if he wanted to arrange many fights for me. I was slowly repaying Catherine, and all of us were eating regularly, so things were looking up. Platner got me fights against all comers in my weight division. I had another fight with Eddie Booker, the boy I fought just before going into the hospital, and again it was a ten-round draw.

A rematch was made with Jack Chase for the State Middleweight Championship, to be held at Lane Field. It drew about 3000 people and I made $740. It went the full fifteen rounds. We fought in the afternoon, and as the sun began to go down I thought about some of the old-time fighters who used ring maneuvers to keep their opponents constantly turned towards the sun. I kept Chase facing the sun all through the afternoon, and when the sun went down Chase's eyes were so tight I had no trouble with him and won at the end of fifteen. That was on May 8, 1943, but after fighting Eddie Cerda, K.O. in three, Big Boy Hogue, K.O. in five, I again fought Chase in San Francisco and lost the decision. I not only lost; he knocked me down twice and I am sure there was very little sun that night. I think Chase was smart enough to have figured out my style, for he easily won nine of the fifteen rounds.

I always liked Chase and thought he was a very good fighter, but we met in the ring three more times and I won two and one was a draw. The last fight was a slaughter, and I knocked him out in the ninth round.

I had been hounding Platner for a championship fight, but after losing to Chase in San Francisco I had to bark more quietly. I still wanted a big-time fight. Ken Overlin was ready to fight in Kansas for a promoter named Frankie Gatto, and I wanted to be matched against Overlin but Platner said it couldn't be done. I don't suppose they could come to terms, or perhaps Platner didn't think I was ready for Overlin at that time.

The Chase fight brought in about $1000, and I got approximately half. The usual training expenses, my own living, the support at home and repaying Catherine left me with little, and I was financially discouraged. All these things cut into my perfection of relaxism, but I was getting there. I would sit at home and pick up the paper only to read of fighters like Jake LaMotta drawing houses of $60,000 and Sugar Ray Robinson getting a $90,000 purse against George Costa in Chicago, and I knew, even in those days, I was just as good if not better than those fellows. Of course Robinson was then a welterweight.

I kept nagging Platner, with no result. And to add to all of my aggravation my wife returned, having decided we should try again. At this time it was a foregone conclusion that Catherine and I would marry, but Catherine believed Mattie was sincere and thought she was entitled to try and patch up the differences between us. Catherine stepped aside, and Mattie and I moved in with Felix. I had convinced myself that I was the villain who had broken up our marriage, but I now truly believe the Pacific Ocean was the heavy. Such a long separation after so short a marriage made a courtship into a friendship, and finally, in this rematch, into a Donnybrook. We were constantly arguing, although neither of us was conscious of who started which fight or why. The tension was there, and to this day I can't explain it. There was nothing wrong with Mattie and, as far as I know, nothing too wrong with me. But a clash of personality is just that and nothing more, and should be dissolved or resolved as quickly as possible. We separated again and I was fidgety and wanted a change of scene. Felix Thurman suggested we move on up the coast to Oakland, outside San Francisco, where fighting was better. I had fought on the first card Jimmy Murray had promoted in Frisco and thought he would help me get matched, I was still technically under contract to Linn Platner's brother but Linn was an understanding man and he wished me well, so we made our plans. I bought, with a $35 down payment, a 1935 Dodge panel truck. It looked like a hearse. It was a one-ton truck big enough to put an icebox and double mattress inside. We added our bed clothes, our wardrobe and my boxing equipment, and we set up housekeeping as we rolled up the coast from San Diego to Oakland.

After beating Yolande Pompey in London, I went to the Derby at Epsom Downs. I'm not a betting man, but you can't wear these clothes alone in a hotel.

KEYSTONE PRESS

I've been teaching Sunday school most of my life and, when I visited Sydney, Australia, in 1940, I was invited to speak in the church I attended. I didn't need my diet in my amateur days. Yeah, that's me on the right, (below).

Here's three of a kind that won the pot for me: Joey Maxim, who held the Light Heavyweight Title prior to meeting me; next, Harold Johnson, number one contender, who's still number one but not the champ. Decked at bottom is Bobo Olson. Winning this fight earned me the fight with Rocky Marciano.

WIDE WORLD PHOTOS

WIDE WORLD PHOTOS

WIDE WORLD PHOTOS

WIDE WORLD PHOTOS

WIDE WORLD PHOTOS

Playing "tag" with the Heavyweight Champ isn't as much fun as it seems to be. The gate for this fight went over a million dollars with the ancillary rights counted in. After the fight I visited a night club and played a little bass. Isn't that a contagious wink I developed? I play piano, too, but will shoot some pool with tone-deaf guests. After all, a man can't spend his whole life just fightin' n' fiddlin'.

WIDE WORLD PHOTOS

Floyd Patterson has just hit me with a left hook, so let's change the subject, and glance down at Yvon Dutelle as he hits the deck in our sensational fight that gave me the world's record for most knockouts. I did it again and achieved 208 K.O.'s.

AP WIREPHOTO—WIDE WORLD PHOTOS

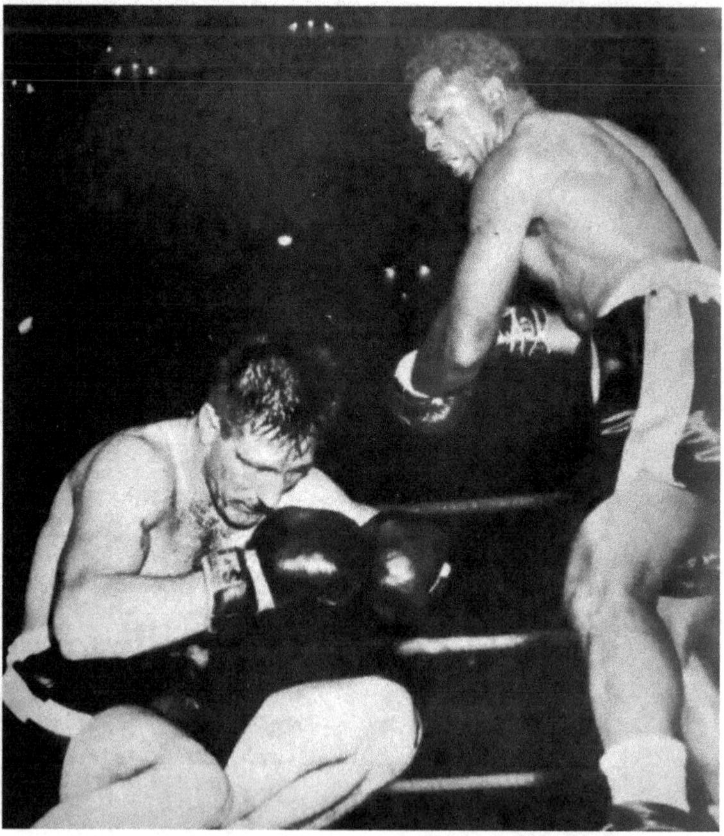

WIDE WORLD PHOTOS

Every man should have a hobby, and I'm afraid eating is just a hobby to a prize fighter. Here's how to be a hobby horse.

*The Adventures of Huckleberry Finn*, M-G-M

Eddie Hodges and I cool our hot dogs on the set of Huckleberry Finn. That's Tony Randall, "the King," in regal attire, demonstrating the royal way to fry an egg to his attentive, if damp, court.

*The Adventures of Huckleberry Finn*, M-G-M

*The Adventures of Huckleberry Finn,* M-G-M

My wife Joan brought the baby Joanie and big girl Rena to visit at MGM. Meanwhile, back at the ranch, the Salt Mine basks quietly in the noonday sun. It's siesta time when I'm in training.

BILL GILLOHM

# ROUND 7 IN THE TANK

A man's home is his castle, and mine had three forward speeds and a reverse. I had a saxophone with a leaky valve, and I would serenade Felix when we pulled off the road to get a night's sleep. When we arrived in Oakland our problem was to park our castle where it would be practical. Felix suggested driving to the heart of town and finding a parking lot where we could make a monthly deal. We'd park near the gym and save carfare. It sounded like a fabulous idea, for we had no carfare to begin with. We stopped at the corner of Tenth and Franklin Streets at a service station owned and operated by a fellow named Mike Segal, who was a former boxer and had heard of me. I explained we were up in Oakland looking for fights. If I couldn't get a fight immediately we intended to look for jobs in the shipyards. I was now twenty-three and Felix was about forty-eight. Surgery had settled the draft question for me. Segal innocently asked what hotel we were going to stay at, and I pointed at the truck and said the hotel Dodge. We opened the rear of the truck and gave him a full Ed Murrow tour of our home. He must have been impressed, for he suggested we park the truck right at the service station beside a wall. He tendered us the key to the washroom and after much debate the nominal rent of $1 a month was decided upon. We now had a home, a fashionable address and a key to the toilet.

I began training. I trained as hard as any man ever has for thirty days, doing roadwork in Merritt Park in the morning and working out in the gym in the afternoon. The both of us lived on a dollar and a half a day. Felix had been going to the shipyard looking for a job and soon he landed one as a welder. Please remember that Felix had a family to support back in San Diego, just as I did, so his getting a job didn't raise our standard of living. We went on, eating like fools on 75 cents a day.

Once Felix started working, he had to get up before I did. He'd rise at five in the morning and travel 20 miles to Richmond and I wouldn't get up until six or six-thirty. Each morning, as he prepared to leave the Hotel Dodge, he would take 75 cents and put it on the ledge that ran around the inside of the truck. When I woke up the first thing I did was to grope for the food money on a signal from my stomach.

One morning Felix rose as usual and I heard him leave the truck. I was half asleep but I groped for my daily stipend and it wasn't there. I was wide awake in an instant and I couldn't figure out why he hadn't left the money. I didn't know that although Felix was on the payroll, he hadn't drawn his first pay as yet and just that morning he had run out of money. I later learned his intention was to borrow against his check, but he'd still have to go to the job to do that and meanwhile what was I to do about eating?

Felix and I had been pestering Jim Murray, the Oakland promoter, about getting a fight for me, but he seemed to use everybody and his brother but not Archie Moore. I had beaten several good fighters and had won the light heavyweight title of the state and I felt I deserved a fight. I had helped Jim Murray get his start when he came up from Los Angeles. I had boxed on his first card against Jimmy Casino. I remember it was my third fight after my operation and I won by a knockout in five rounds. It was, and is, my feeling that he was obligated to do me a good turn, but he didn't do it. This aggravation on top of my not having breakfast money caused me to steam and set back my relaxism more than somewhat.

I was peeved and I was sulking. I didn't know what to do. No future fight in sight and I couldn't even eat breakfast. It's impossible to train on an empty stomach. It would be foolish to do roadwork and build up an even greater appetite. I felt myself getting hungrier and hungrier. And angrier and angrier. When Mike Segal arrived I didn't even ask him for a quarter for breakfast. I'd been through too much in life to beg or borrow, especially from a man who had been so nice to us with a token rent of a dollar a month. He was curious when he saw me sitting on the tailgate and asked why I wasn't out running. I merely said I didn't feel like running. He chatted on about a day off not hurting anyone, as I looked to be in great shape. I was. I was down to about 155 pounds, and going down by the minute.

I sat and dreamed about the good old Loose-Wiles Biscuit Company in St. Louis. I mentally ate a bag of broken cookies. I thought about the lucky aborigines who were then chewing on succulent eucalyptus leaves plucked from trees set 5 miles apart. I thought of the meals I had had on board ship and the thousands of pounds of food I had shunned during my training life. I thought of Auntie's fried chicken and almost cried. I concentrated on food.

Very often, after returning from roadwork, I'd give Mike a very small hand around the service station, but that morning I just sat, dejected, as he went about his work. Even gas smelled like gravy that morning. Tires looked tender. It got to be about eight o'clock when I noticed a boy coming down the street. He was cheerily whistling and looked as though he didn't have a care in the world. He called out a merry greeting to me and I waved to him although I was aware the effort would make me hungrier. We were about the same age. He thought my face was familiar but when I told him my name his face remained blank and I knew he wasn't a boxing fan. He said he thought he knew me from Chicago but I told him that couldn't be. He lived in Chicago and was a waiter on a train. On impulse I asked if there were any jobs open on the railroad, as the one place I wanted to be right at that moment was inside a dining car with a license to steal. He told me to go to the railroad yard at the foot of Fifth Street and anybody around there would point out the employment office. When I arrived there, I found fifty or sixty men ahead of me, but I sat down, as I had no place to go and I wanted to see what went on. Every now and then a man would enter this big room and call out, "Give me two chefs!" And two men got up and followed him out. "I want three number twos! " And so on. Each time he yelled some men would follow him out. They all seemed to have credentials of some kind. I decided to wait until the man yelled and no one stood up. I figured that would be the job for Archie. Finally he appeared and said, "I need a fourth cook! " I looked around and no one moved, so I stood up and followed him. I thought I could surely be a fourth cook, and if I sat there much longer all the jobs would be gone. With my fast jab I figured to spear breakfast before I got fired for incompetence. As I answered the call, several of the men smiled at me and I didn't know why. But then I didn't know what a fourth cook was. The man I followed handed me a uniform and told me what track my train was making up on, and I left.

The train was due to leave at eleven o'clock, and I got on board and saw some of the men who had been hired ahead of me. I entered the dining car, and everybody seemed to know what they had to do except me. The nickname for the fourth cook was "Forty" and when the bossman called me I didn't know who he was talking to. He came over and asked me pleasantly if I had ever worked in a dining car before. I said no. He suggested I step into the kitchen, and the aroma from that tiny mecca beckoned me like the Holy Grail. I thought I'd have to peel potatoes and scrape carrots but when I mentioned this he grinned and said, "No, boy. You've got to jump in the tank." He pointed to the dish tank, steaming and appealing, and I realized I was face to face with my first and only tank job.

I stayed in the dish tank from Oakland, California, to Ogden, Utah. I had my head bent over that tank except for brief intervals to eat and sleep from one railroad yard to another. The train was a soldier's special, and as soon as one meal was over another began. If they had thrown dirty dishes at the enemy the war would have been over much sooner. At first, because of the soldiers, I felt I was not only earning a living but doing a patriotic duty, but I soon felt that not even German soldiers could be that mean. I began to worry about Archie Moore the fighter suffering from dishpan hands, and I tried to think of everything but food. The smell of food was in my skin, my clothes, and it was overwhelming. I couldn't believe I had ever been hungry and wanted to rush out into the dining area and plead with the men to lay down their knives and forks, as I was sure they didn't know what I knew and that they were killing themselves by eating. For two long weeks I was tanked up, and when the train finally rolled into the Ogden yard I had a couple of days off. Dining-car men slept in the dining car, for the tables ingeniously folded into beds. Most of the regular men played cards or talked during the night, as they took time off at the end of a run. I wanted to make money, so I immediately turned round and went back. But after two weeks I needed some time off. I met a friend of mine named Raymond Brown from Indianapolis. We had gone to school together. He asked me if I knew a fellow named Archie Moore was making quite a name for himself on the West Coast as a fighter. He told me he had been following this guy's career, thinking it was me. I told him to get transferred to my train and he could follow Archie Moore's career much closer, as I didn't want to lose a good fan over a trivial matter of two hundred or so dirty dishes.

The train crews, of course, knew who I was. Most Negro fight fans take great pride in Negro fighters, for it is surely one field of American endeavor where race means nothing and the better man can win solely on merit. These men were delighted to have me working with them and thought nothing of my menial job, as all of them had suffered reverses at one time or another. They used to kid me in a good-natured way. I had been saving almost every penny I got hold of and I didn't draw any pay. I just wanted to get a stake to last me until I could get back to Oakland and get a match. I knew I couldn't go on washing dishes forever. Knew it? Man, I was sure of it.

I had finally gotten used to the kitchen odors and my appetite returned. You can live high off the hog in a dining car, but the hard work kept me from gaining weight. My hands were actually getting exceedingly soft in the hot water but I thought I could remedy that by soaking them in brine when I got off the train. The waiters gave me a share of their tips. I wasn't lazy, and having clean dishes always ready did improve the service, so the boys liked me and I liked them. They provided me with a pocketful of dimes that I spent in Ogden.

I shot some pool, saw a movie or two and took an occasional whirl in a penny ante crap game. I lived on the train and when I stayed a night or two in Ogden, the railroad issued me "paper" good at a hotel near the yard. When I arrived in Oakland on one trip I felt I had had it, so I drew my pay and said goodbye to my train mates. I had nearly a hundred dollars and a full stomach.

I immediately went to the service station to see Mike Segal and was surprised to find the truck was gone. I wondered about my boxing equipment. Mike told me where I could find Felix, who had moved to a hotel, and was about to leave to see him when Mike stopped me, saying a telegram had arrived for me the day before. It was from Platner, and he wanted to match me with Shorty Hogue in San Diego.

I found Felix and discovered he had brought his wife and daughter up to Oakland, that all three were now working at the shipyard, and their combined income was over $300 a week. This meant he was through with the fight game. They worked hard during the war, and the Thurman family saved enough money to buy property in San Diego, which they still own.

I had one unfinished piece of business. The finance company wanted the rest of the money for the truck. Felix told me he had lent it to a man named Bevo, who had parked it near the shipyard and was living in it. I told Felix to tell him he'd have to make other arrangements, because I would have to tell the finance company where the truck was so they could repossess it. Felix had removed my personal effects from the truck, so I was packed and ready to go back to San Diego.

I boarded the first train I could catch and, as it was almost dinner time, I wandered into the dining car and sat luxuriously at ease at a table with a gleaming white cloth, and I was served a meal by a pleasant waiter whom I tipped lavishly. He called me Mr. Moore and served me on shiny, clean plates.

# ROUND 8 JOEY NOT CHLOE

In San Diego, in 1942, I opened my Chicken Shack. I continued to fight but kept the shack open as a steady business, which boxing certainly was not. I fought up and down the West Coast from '42 to '44 and then decided to go back East. But before I made my move my brother Louis came West to live with me and work in the shack.

Louis was born to get into trouble. He had continued his gambling but had switched from marbles to money. He had taught himself to palm cards and switch dice and generally cut corners on slightly illegal projects, and my mother, who was then living in St. Louis, wrote and asked me to send for him. He was a natural boxer and I had always hoped he would turn to professional fighting, but rigorous training didn't appeal to him. I drove to the station in Los Angeles, as I was fighting in Hollywood the next night. I waited on the platform for about twenty minutes until everyone had gotten off the train, and was about to walk away when Louis appeared. He had been hiding and had been amused at my running back and forth along the train looking for him.

I could see he hadn't changed much, and when I got back to San Diego I put him in school. After about four days the truant officer came to see me and asked me why Louis wasn't going to school. I was amazed, as I believed he was going every day. He had been playing hookey right along. I tried to talk to Louis and explain the value of an education, but he wanted no part of school. He said he wanted to work with me, and since he was now sixteen and could quit I let him. I gave him a job as dish washer. I was the waiter, cashier and general handyman and I had a cook named Tiny. He was twenty years old and wanted to be a fighter, and he worked for me in between his fights. Louis, now going on seventeen, seemed to be a juvenile delinquent in Tiny's eyes, and they didn't get along at all. Tiny would make vague threats that someday he'd shake Louis up. Louis finally told Tiny to stop talking and go into action, but Tiny maintained that if he hit Louis I would retaliate, and since I was a well-known professional he wouldn't have a chance. All this conversation came back to me, and I thought a good shaking up was what Louis needed, so I told the two of them that we'd go to the gym in the morning and I'd referee the bout. So the next morning off we went, and if they were still fighting today Tiny would still be trying to hit Louis. My young brother pummeled poor Tiny and made a fool of him, so much so that I stopped the fight after two rounds. Now Louis grinned at Tiny and said, "You were gonna put me in my place but couldn't. So I'll put you in my place instead." And right there he made Tiny the dishwasher and he became the cook. He was a very talented chicken fryer, too.

But Louis was light-fingered by nature and somehow a man's watch got tangled up in his hand, and the man sent the police to ask Louis what time it was. I appeared in court and got Louis paroled in my custody, and then decided to drive him back to St. Louis. I wanted to visit my aunt, who had moved back to St. Louis, and I could redeposit Louis with our mother. Auntie wrote that Mother had moved to Pittsburgh, but I had made up my mind to make the trip anyway, and a friend and I packed Louis and the baggage and off we went. When we reached St. Louis, Louis just vanished and I had to leave without him. I was going on to New York. Mr. Platner had arranged for me to meet the late Jimmy Johnston, the Madison Square Garden matchmaker. First he contacted Al Weill, who later managed Rocky Marciano, but Mr. Platner didn't like his attitude towards Negro fighters and wouldn't send me to him.

My aunt and my mother were upset about my leaving St. Louis without my brother, but I was in a hurry and no one knew where he was. Louis finally got to Pittsburgh on his own, but he still acted as though he was in sunny California and the weather in Pittsburgh was quite cold. He went bareheaded and wore his shirt open at the collar and generally didn't wear the proper clothing. He contracted tubercular pneumonia, and my mother called me in New York to ask me to come to Pittsburgh. I had a fight scheduled with Odell Riley for November 12, 1945, and sent my mother a telegram saying I had to go to Detroit to make this bout. Riley was rated number eight among the heavyweights at the time and he had just defeated Lee Q. Murray. I called from Detroit and said I'd leave right after the fight, but later that day I got a wire saying Louis had died.

I couldn't get to the funeral, because I thought it more important to fight and make some money, as the funeral would have to be paid for. He had often joked with me, saying that if he died he wanted to be buried in my sports jacket, a gaudy Harris tweed. Even that I remembered too late, so Louis was buried after eighteen years of sheer fun with absolutely no responsibilities. I'll always remember Louis for the fun he generated wherever he was.

I'm afraid I fought Riley with a little more savageness than usual. I knocked him out cold at the end of the third round but his seconds, who were feeling fine, revived him and sent him out for the fourth. I knocked him out again in the sixth round and, like a bullfighter, I dedicated this win to Louis.

Let me pick up my story of going to New York to see Mr. Johnston. My buddy and I drove to Indianapolis, where I looked up Hiawatha Grey and asked him if he would like to come to New York with me as my trainer, for it looked as if Mr. Johnston would be getting me some good fights. But Hiawatha was training George Costner then, and turned the offer down. Costner went on to fight LaMotta, and then had a $90,000 gate with Sugar Ray. I left Hiawatha with Costner and went on to Pittsburgh. We were sailing along at about 70 miles an hour when engine trouble developed, the car overheated and it threw a rod. I walked 4 miles to the next town, Bedford, and ordered a new engine for the car. Luckily we caught a local bus to New York and so the delay wasn't too bad. That engine cost me $439.

As soon as I arrived in New York, I went to the Paramount Building at Times Square where Mr. Johnston had his office. Jimmy was a cocky little fellow who wore a derby jauntily tilted forward on his head. Jimmy didn't smoke or drink, but he was a colorful character on Broadway. He welcomed me and told me he'd find fights for me, and I was to report to the gymnasium the next morning and start training. I explained what had happened to the car and told him I had no money. He cheerfully gave me $25 and said he'd give me the same every week, and that he would pay the fee at Stillman's gymnasium on Eighth Avenue.

At Stillman's I met many "name" fighters and many more who were destined to go on to fame and glory in my profession. Sandy Saddler was just beginning about then, and we became fast friends. I met Jake LaMotta and Steve Lawless and we'd talk in the dressing rooms or over a cup of coffee, and we began to discuss ways and means of organizing fighters. But fighters are great individuals, and organizing them was not easy. In fact it was impossible. The fight managers organized before we could make a move.

Jimmy Johnston, being a matchmaker, couldn't be my manager of record, so I signed a contract with his brother Charley. I was scheduled to fight in Boston and I was the semi-windup on the card. I boxed against a big fellow named Nap Mitchell who stood 6 feet 4 and weighed 210 pounds. He was out of Philadelphia. Looking at him across the ring made an impression on me, but I got up at the bell and went out as I had agreed to do. He wasn't able to hit me but I was able to hit him. This added up in my favor, so I knocked him out in the sixth round. This was my fourth fight since coming East, and I won three by knockouts and one by decision. I was beginning to roll, but other managers avoided me.

I was making the same mistake I had made on my last trip to New York. I would work out with men heavier than me and out of my division—heavyweights like Teddy Randolph and Lee Oma—and my showing against these men was so good fighters in my division were hesitant about fighting me. The lighter fighters used to love to watch me spar with people like Kid Coco and Jimmy Doyle. Saddler, Paddy Young and Paddy DeMarco and Tony Palone used to study my style. The Johnston brothers had quite a stable of tigers then, but I was the star attraction at Stillman's. Rocky Graziano was around at that time and Rocky was getting a nice build-up, while I was getting a freeze. He became the title holder in the middleweight class.

Before going to Boston I had a fight in the St. Nick Arena, which, in those days, was one short step below the Garden. The Garden, of course, was to boxing what the old Palace was to vaudeville. I was matched against Bob Jacobs, a Philadelphia boy, and wanted to win so I could fight in the Garden as a main event and collect a nice payday. At that time the Garden gate averaged about $60,000, as these were the war years and sporting events were generally doing big business.

The day of the fight I discovered I had no money. I hadn't kept to my budget, and the day before I had carfare back to Harlem where I was living and not a red cent more. So I walked from 147$^{th}$ Street down to the Paramount Building at 44$^{th}$ Street and Broadway. I just made it and met Johnston coming out looking for a cab, and he invited me to go along to the commissioner's office for the weighing-in. I hadn't eaten since the night before, and the long walk had sharpened my appetite. At the time I was an overstuffed middleweight and was beginning to campaign as a light heavyweight, and I weighed in at 165 pounds. Bob Jacobs weighed 175. Johnston gave me some money and I got a nice steak and a glass of orange juice and I went on to the arena. It wasn't a dull fight, but it was a safe fight. Nothing spectacular and nothing sensational. I knocked Jacobs out in the ninth round, but my showing wasn't at all impressive and there was barely a mention in the papers. It took the steam out of my chances for a shot in the Garden right away.

Now Johnston rematched me with Nate Boland. My first New York fight had been against Boland, whose home town was Baltimore. I had won the first fight by a decision in ten rounds, and the rematch was held in Baltimore, where Boland was a great favorite. Once again we went ten rounds to a decision, and once again I won. We were both talented boxers and it was a good fight to watch, although most fight crowds seem to enjoy slugging matches with fighters like Graziano and LaMotta. But this win over Boland established me as a draw in Baltimore. I had a total of twenty fights in Baltimore through the years and lost only one.

My second fight in Baltimore was with Teddy Randolph, the boy who used to work out with me at Stillman's. He was a good puncher and a crowd-pleaser. The fight started with both of us feeling the other out, although we were very familiar with each other's style. Teddy had his mother and girlfriend at ringside, I am sorry to say, because before long many of the ringsiders were splattered with blood and Teddy collapsed from exhaustion and from the beating I was giving him in the ninth round.

From Randolph to Maxim is but six years, seventy-two fights with six losses. In 1949 I had thirteen fights and won ten by knockouts. I was disgusted. I couldn't get a shot at the title. In 1950 I fought only twice and made a living with my pool cue, hustling for small bets in neighborhood pool rooms in whatever town I was in. After fighting Lloyd Marshall in Cleveland on June 26, 1946, I was the leading contender for the light heavyweight title, and remained number one for five years with the exception of one month. In that time, I fought Ezzard Charles three times and lost to him three times. In looking at the record book it would seem that Ezzard likes me as his "cousin," which is a term baseball players use. A great hitter is constantly struck out by an obscure pitcher and no one can figure it. Ball players call them "cousins." I'm not saying Charles was an obscure boxer. Far from it. But somehow he had my number. I felt

I beat him in our first fight but the record is there; it says he beat me. In our second he was on his home ground and I really thought I was robbed. Sports writers agreed with me, but the record says I lost in ten rounds. After the third fight Charles told me he never wanted to fight me again. So be it. But I am down in cold print as never having beat the guy.

I was the leading contender through the reigns of three champions: Freddie Mills of England, Gus Lesnevich and Joey Maxim. When Maxim won the title I really began to campaign in earnest. Jack Kearns was Maxim's manager, and a more elusive man is hard to find. My own manager wasn't much help. When Jimmy Johnston died his brother Charley took over the managerial chores full-time, but the affection I had for Jimmy didn't extend to Charley and never has. I knew that he and Doc Kearns were old friends, and it was a mystery to me why we couldn't all get together on a title fight. But Charley said Kearns was a long time between big paydays, and we should give him a chance to earn some money with Maxim. The one thing Johnston did agree with me on was that I could beat Maxim. Doc Kearns came out of the Klondike and had been a fighter himself years before. He's been the manager of ten champions, including Jack Dempsey and Mickey Walker. He'd been a big moneymaker before I was born. I think Charley and Doc was closer than records in a juke box. Today, Doc acts as my agent from fight to fight. End of story. I was fighting for peanuts, and Charley would smile and bank it after explaining how high my expenses were.

I took matters in my own hands, as much as I could. I began a letter-writing campaign to sports writers all over the country. I pleaded, I cursed, I demanded a shot at Maxim's crown. The boys on the sports desk were great, but not a one of them was a matchmaker. Meanwhile my manager kept reminding me how old Joe Walcott was when he got a title shot. I believe Charley Johnston thinks I have the mind of a four-year-old. At that I must have been fairly simple to have him for a manager. But time actually gave me a double blessing, for not many fighters can boast of having both Johnston and Kearns telling them what to do.

Mr. Eddie Eagan was commissioner of boxing in New York State. I ran into him accidentally in the lobby of Madison Square Garden. He had been a great amateur light heavyweight and I thought he would be in sympathy with my plea. I approached him and told him who I was and what I wanted. He almost snapped my head off with a surly reply, saying he was a commissioner and not a matchmaker. I have been brushed off in my day but usually I've been left standing. He swept me aside like a bread crumb on a waiter's tip. Here was a man whose salary was paid by the public to insure decent practices in boxing and he wouldn't give me the time of day. They lifted my title for not defending in six months (I was reinstated soon after), but for six years I couldn't get a sniff at it. Mr. Robert Christenberry became commissioner and I wrote him a long letter stating my grievances. He wrote back a most sympathetic letter, saying the same things that Eagan had said, but this time it was nice hearing from a gentleman.

Now my contract with Johnston was about to expire and I was thinking of a suitable going-away present for Charley when he suddenly called and said he had arranged a match with Maxim. I was sure he had dialed a wrong number but the conversation was confirmed later. The one fly in the ointment was the contract. Charley didn't come right out and mention it but he was chewing his food more carefully in those days. So on December 17, 1952, four days after my thirty-sixth birthday, I was to fight Joey Maxim for the title.

You could give Doc Kearns 200 pounds of steel wool and he'd knit you a stove. He was knitting furiously a few days before the Maxim fight, because Charley Johnston brought up the matter of contract the night before the big event. He told me Kearns was threatening to call the fight off unless I signed a new agreement giving a piece of me to Kearns. Johnston stayed in the deal. Not realizing Kearns was actually powerless to stop the fight and being so eager to fight for the title, I agreed and I signed the new pact. Where, oh where, is Mr. Lincoln?

I had waived all interest in money to get this bout. I knew I could win and I thought the title would pay off after the fight. But now Charley and Kearns were partners, so the only loser was me. I made about $800 winning the World's Championship. Kearns had demanded and gotten a $100,000 guarantee. The gate was $89,000 and TV brought in more than $50,000 more. The fight itself was the only satisfactory thing. I won thirteen out of fifteen rounds and it was a clean decision. My "old friend" from the St. Louis days, Harry Kessler, was the referee. He gave me the decision by only two points, while the other judges were unanimously in my favor. And even after this, Johnston didn't protest when Kessler was announced as referee in my fight with Marciano. When the fight ended I moved across the ring to speak to Maxim. I was stopped when Kearns stepped in and said to me, "Never mind the condolences, kid; we've got all the money." I wanted to reply that I'd gotten the title but that seemed foolish inasmuch as Kearns had me, too.

I took the $800 and paid off my sparring partners and learned that Johnston had borrowed $10,000 from the I.B.C. against the return match with Maxim.

On June 24, 1953, in Ogden, Utah, I fought Maxim for the second time. Ogden is a good fight town, and many years before, Kearns had sent Jack Dempsey into action there. As a publicity stunt, the weighing-in ceremonies were held on stage in a theater for the TV and newsreel cameras. After the weigh-in, the referee, Ray Miller, was to give us our instructions. He is a potential Barrymore. He carried on like a religious fanatic and I finally had to point out to him that both Maxim and myself had fought at least once before this and had a fair knowledge of the rules. I don't think Miller cares for me very much, as I spoiled his screen test. I beat Maxim after fifteen rounds in a grueling contest. He was a fine opponent.

I now felt I was truly champion after seventeen years of working at my trade. I could now pay off some old scores. I wasn't bitter but I was getting choosy about my company. People who had put the knock on me throughout the years now came fawning around, and

I must say it was a pleasure to ignore them. Kearns and Johnston got together, and if those two ever decided to go into fund-raising work, the banks would all close. They decided to match me a third time against Maxim. I was on my first South American tour when I had heard of getting my shot at Maxim originally, and now I was in South America again.

The first time I visited South America I was invited along as an extra attraction in the Johnston menagerie. Sandy Saddler, the featherweight champion, was the star.

Saddler and I were very good friends and I believe I helped him win the title from Willie Pep.

I was at Saddler's training camp for three weeks before the title match. I ate, slept, walked and talked with Sandy every day. Sandy was a very superstitious man, of West Indian extraction. One day, for example, Sandy had a sore hand and visited a "faith healer," who rubbed oil on Sandy's hand and blessed it. Immediately the hand felt better. Sandy believed in things like this, and they helped him. He was a bit worried about fighting Pep, who was one of the great men of boxing, and I concocted an idea to give him back his confidence. The morning of the fight I knocked on his door at seven and told Sandy I had something important to tell him.

"Sandy," I said, "you have just won the featherweight title of the world by a knockout in four rounds."

"Did I?" he said incredulously.

"Yes, you did," I replied. "You know what you did? You knocked him down in the second round. You knocked him down again in the third round and you knocked him out in the fourth." I explained that I often had visions, and I would go over the fight in detail as we did our morning roadwork. He was excited and got dressed, and we trotted along for about a mile, as I related the fight punch by punch until the knockout. Now I knew Pep had been having trouble making the weight, and so I knew he would go to the weigh-in early. Fighters who have trouble making the weight invariably do that, so they can get a test weigh on the scales before the official weighing-in. I told Sandy that we would go to the weigh-in at the last possible moment.

"When you see Pep," I told him, "keep your hands in your pockets and if he speaks to you just mumble at him and keep moving. When they pose you after the weigh-in for the newspaper photographers, grip his hand as hard as you can and look him in the eye. Make him break his gaze first, stare him down."

Sandy did exactly what I told him, and when we left the weighing-in ceremonies I assured him he had the fight won. I told him to stare Pep down again when he went to the middle of the ring for the referee's instructions, and he did. This was an old trick of mine, which I had used in many fights, and still use. Pep was a great boxer, and he had a knack of spinning his opponents, then hitting them hard when they were off balance. I showed Sandy how to snap Pep's head forward with his left hand and then hit hard with a right uppercut. Follow that with a quick jab and Pep would do the spinning. Sandy won just as I had predicted, in the fourth round.

Johnston made a good deal in bringing both Saddler and myself to South America. It was good from his point of view for two reasons. The dollar exchange was perfect for us, and the farther away from Maxim I was the better he liked it. I had eight fights on that first trip, won seven by knockouts and fought one draw. I was very popular with the fight crowd down there, and I had my own system of public relations and good will. We traveled from town to town, and in each town we visited I would pick out an underprivileged kid and dress him from the skin out. We were making a lot of money, and I could well afford this and enjoyed doing it. However, like everything else that happened in Argentina, Juan Peron heard about it, and our entire entourage was invited to meet him at the palace. Eva Peron was a boxing enthusiast, and she told me she thought I was the cleverest boxer she had ever seen. I saw a great deal of Peron, and he lent me his yacht and crew for a sightseeing trip. My South American agent, Robert D'Angelo, saw to it that I met many important people in Argentina, but I was criticized for being so friendly to Peron. I am not a political person, and when the head of a government invites me to meet him I think it judicious to do so. I was a representative of America and an athlete, and I felt excited about being asked. Jack Dempsey met him, as did Charley Johnston and Sandy Saddler, but I was the one chastised by the State Department. I imagine publicity pictures of me filtered back, and so I was singled out. I don't defend Peron, nor do I condemn him, for I must judge people as individuals and by their relationship to me. He treated me very cordially, and that was that.

My second trip to South America was even greater. I was now El Champion, and the toast of the country. One incident stands out. I was making an exhibition tour and boxed in small towns, in prisons, at universities. One night in a restaurant a tall, strapping blond guy politely approached me and asked where I was fighting next. I told him and he asked if he could fight with me. I shrugged and said sure. D'Angelo said the man wasn't a known fighter; he had never heard of him. The following night I was boxing in Sunchales, a small town in the interior, when down the aisle to the ring came the blond giant. He was wearing trunks and had his gloves on. I was scheduled to fight three rounds each against two opponents and was quite surprised to see this fellow show up. The same girl who had been with him the night before was with him now. He climbed into the ring and ever so politely asked when I would want him. He was a big guy and an unknown quantity, so I decided to battle him first. In about two seconds I knew he had never fought before, so I pulled a right hand haymaker from the floor and telegraphed it so that even a blind man would have seen it coming. It caught him flush on the chin and lifted him off the floor and onto his back. His girl was duly impressed, and later that night they joined us and his girl was beaming over her boyfriend's courage. Years later, after the first Durelle fight, I was approached by a writer from *Sports Illustrated* who was doing a series. He had pitched to a big-league team, he had played tennis against a Davis Cup champ, he had practiced with a pro football team, and so forth. What he wanted to do was fight me three rounds. I reluctantly agreed. I don't like to fight amateurs, as they may, through inexperience, stick a thumb in your eye, or you could break a hand. I make my living fighting, and it isn't a hobby with me. The writer, George Plimpton, made a date and we met at Stillman's gym. I thought a few people plus a photographer would be there, but a few hundred of Plimpton's friends were on hand. I don't know whether they came to see him get a shellacking or to cheer him on, but I found the whole episode a bit embarrassing. I naturally didn't want to hurt him and yet I didn't want to look like a fool. He said he had boxed in college, a remark that made Doc Kearns say, "Yes, but answer the question, do you know how to fight?" I told George to fire away and I would defend myself. In self-defense I'm afraid I unintentionally hurt George a bit, although I was trying to block his punches, and not even hit him. George was game and later, when I dressed, I saw him sitting on a stool, being a bit sick to his stomach with his nose bleeding, so I slapped him on the back and said, "Don't forget. You're entitled to a rematch."

I have been to South America a total of five times and I hope to go back on an exhibition tour in the future. The people like me and I like them. But now I was back in the United States getting ready to fight Maxim for the third time.

The fight was set for January 27, 1954. It was to be held in Miami. Doc Kearns, being manager of both fighters, had access to both training camps. Being that Doc is a sentimentalist about money, I think he would have liked Maxim to win, because then he could have arranged still another rematch. As it was, I was getting a little weary of fighting Joey. For so many years I couldn't get near him, and now I couldn't get away from him. Kearns visited my camp and gleefully juggled my scales a bit. With my system for reducing I check my weight several times a day. Everything seemed fine, but at the weigh-in the day before the fight I stepped on the official scales and was horrified to see I was 5 pounds overweight. I had to go out and do roadwork in the broiling Florida sun to knock off the extra weight. But Doc is a great hand for practical jokes, and I weighed in a second time and made the proper weight, so I forgot about it.

This fight with Maxim was the best from my point of view. I knocked Maxim down twice, which is a feat not many men have been able to do. He takes a punch about as well as any man I've ever fought, and by knocking him down I scored a personal victory that was most gratifying.

Doc Kearns isn't all bad. He is the oldest living fight manager, and his record proves that he has been around the block a few times. He is the greatest moneymaker of all the managers and has handled ten champions. At my ranch in Romona, California, I have huge rocks with names of people I like painted on them. Doc Kearns has his own rock with the motto, "The World's Greatest Manager" written beneath his name. I have names of sports writers, fighters like Joe Louis, Ray Robinson and others. I looked again the other day and just can't find a rock big enough for Charley Johnston.

After the Marciano fight in the Yankee Stadium on September 21, 1955, a writer met Charley in the corridor leading to my dressing room and he asked Charley if he was going to see how I was. Charley's answer was my moment of truth. He said he didn't care how I was, he was going to see how much we had gotten on the losing end. The sports writer printed the story and Charley is suing him. I believe the writer, and I haven't spoken to Charley Johnston aside from necessity since that day. And his brother was such a nice guy.

Fight managers, by nature, have to be very realistic. One fight can often make or break a fighter, and the manager goes broke with him. Therefore, they try and have more than one basket to carry their eggs in, and Johnston and Kearns are by no means unusual in this respect. Kearns is a moneymaker. He knows how to ballyhoo a fight. There is an old story that he once printed an extra set of tickets for a Dempsey Garden bout and sold the house twice. They say the best fights that night were in the seats. Just how true this story is will never be known, but my hat is off to Doc, for if anybody could do this, he'd be the man.

I hope someone lends Charley Johnston this book. It'd be a shame if he had to spend money for it.

# ROUND 9 FOULED!

Eat spaghetti, kids. Look what spaghetti did for Rocky Marciano. It made him tough enough to take any kind of punch and gave him the strength of a mule. He even had a mule for a manager. A stubborn tough man named Al Weill, who guided his tiger to the heavyweight title, and agreed it was best that he retire undefeated. A manager who can do that has a lot of guts and probably a lot of money.

Rocky Marciano is a good friend of mine. When I last fought Yvon Durelle in August of '59, Rocky paid a visit to my training quarters and we had a nice bull session, posed for some pictures, and he went on his way. It was reported by a New York columnist that he and I had sparred and I had gotten the worst of it. Just think of how ridiculous this was. I was in prime shape, whereas Rocky was bloated and way out of condition. If anybody is foolish enough to think he would get in a ring with me in his condition, they are crazy. For I am very proud of being able to say I dropped Marciano when I fought him, and he was in tip-top condition then. I think I could easily handle him at 200 and some pounds of fat. When Ralph Edwards surprised me by making me the subject of one of his *This Is Your Life* TV shows, Marciano appeared and said then he could still feel the punch I threw at him. That's a nice compliment, and I must admit I can still feel a few of his.

He is a tough man to fight. In my mind there are two kinds of fighters: sluggers and thinkers. Sugar Ray is a rare combination, a thinker and a slugger. A tough combination to beat. But Rocky was pure slugger. Deadly, dangerous at all times. A thinking fighter is harder to figure, even if you are fairly sure you can beat him. He is apt to change tactics and style in the middle of a fight. A slugger never will. A slugger, like Graziano or LaMotta, will take six punches to deliver one. He knows his ability to absorb this kind of punishment and waits for his shot. You can wear yourself out fighting a slugger, but you can get knocked out by a thinker while you're still fresh as a daisy. There is no doubt about Marciano's ability to take a punch. The best have had a shot at him, and he is not too difficult to hit. His ringside manner steadily improved under the tutelage of Charley Goldman, but at best he was never known as a Fancy Dan fighter. When I fought him I considered myself a thinking fighter, but anger changed my tactics and style. I was downright stupid. I began to fight Marciano's fashion, and that was my mistake.

The old saying that coming events cast their shadow beforehand came to be the word of truth, as I look back on the incidents that shaped my getting a chance to fight Rocky and my subsequent loss to Patterson. In Ohio in 1954 I wandered into an auto showroom to buy a car. The business was owned by a man named Bove Reese, who invited me into his office, and we talked about boxing and Archie Moore. It was at a time in my life when I was discouraged. I was in poor shape financially and was disgusted with boxing. I had sold the Chicken Shack to Felix, and was seriously considering buying the car to drive back to San Diego and leave the ring. Bob Reese talked me out of this, and with two friends of his, Dr. Dallis and Mike DiSalle, we planned a publicity barrage to force a title fight for me with Marciano.

At the time I had been palling around with Lucky Thompson, the saxophone player. To make some money and to have something to do, because I thought I was never going to get in the same ring with Rocky, I had made a commitment to tour with his band. This was arranged by a theatrical agent named Herb Bayliss. But Bayliss accepted bookings in advance without consulting Lucky, and he refused to go. My billing in the advertising was so strong I would have been held responsible if the tour fell through. One thing I couldn't use then was a lawsuit, so I decided to go through with the dates booked without Lucky.

I was playing a theater in Cleveland when a woman sent a note backstage asking me to meet her for a cup of coffee after the last show. I met this woman and we had coffee and chatted about mutual friends, and it got to be time to leave. When we parted she casually asked if I had any girlfriends in Cleveland. I said no, as I had been spending most of my time in Toledo prior to the band booking. She offered to introduce me to some girls, and I took her phone number, so I could call when I had an evening free. The band was made up of a group of very friendly guys but none of them were very pretty, so I called and asked her to get me a date. She invited me to her house and called a girl, who seemed anxious to meet me. The woman underestimated how friendly this girl was, and I decided the best place to kill time after theater was in this apartment. After a few visits she suggested that we be friends and do away with all these phone calls. I was wary of any kind of steady arrangement with her, as it seemed to me her morals were a bit shaky. I'm not talking about my own at this point, but at any rate I didn't want to get tied up emotionally or any other way. So we continued as we were, running the phone bill up and new friendly girls dropping by. I was beginning to like the band business.

This woman had a hobby I wasn't aware of. It was home photography, and I caught her snapping a picture of me and immediately confiscated the film from the camera, as my hair wasn't combed and I'm vain about my appearance.

It was late and I was tired and I dozed off. During my snooze, she switched rolls of film, as she was very desirous of having my picture. When I got home I took the roll of film to a friend, who told me it was a fresh roll that had never been exposed, and I knew the trap was set.

On March 9, 1954, I was booked to fight Bob Baker in Miami Beach, and with my music commitments finished I prepared to leave for the South to train. Just before I left, she contacted me and asked for a thousand dollars. It seemed high for a phone bill, so I laughed it off until I received a letter from her, saying my pictures had turned out well indeed, and how many did I want to order? The Valdes and Olson fights were in the offing, and this kind of publicity would have been ruinous. I sent her money.

I suppose apartment life was palling when I was no longer around, because she wrote me, saying she wanted $5000 to build a house. I managed to go and see her and extracted a promise that this $5000 would be the last. It wasn't. She hounded me something fierce.

Time for the Valdes fight rolled around but the examining doctor said I had a heart condition. I had my lady friend to thank for this. They wouldn't allow me to fight. I went from one doctor to another, and in my mind was a statement Al Weill had made that the only time Rocky would fight Archie was when Archie was old enough to be in a wheelchair.

I finally had twenty-seven cardiographs made and it seemed as though there was something the matter. I was admitted to the Ford Hospital, and Dr. John Keyes gave me medication and treatment along with rest, and in a short while I was pronounced sound. I did fight Valdes on May 2, 1955, after a lay-off of more than eight months. Between my ailing heart and my friend I was financially drained. I had neglected training, and fought him weighing 196 pounds. Valdes, of course, was a heavyweight. I beat him in fifteen rounds and my heart held up pretty good. It has since. Knock on wood.

Immediately after Valdes came Olson. This was one of the big wins of my career, and it paved the way for a shot at Marciano. It was the fight that got all the sports writers rooting for me. I gave Bobo the old evil eye and knocked him stiff in three rounds, and was acclaimed the logical challenger to Marciano.

Prior to the Olson fight she must have sensed the well was dry, but she became my number one fan as soon as Olson was tucked in for the night. I had saved the letters she had written and I turned them over to Reese, who was now my business manager, and waited for him to advise me. He said to play along at least until the Marciano fight was in the books. The fight was only seven weeks away, and she was writing daily and calling on the telephone for money, money, money. My ignorance of the law was abysmal and I played it the way Reese had told me to. I sent some money but I stalled as much as I could. I took his advice as gospel.

My training quarters were at North Adams, Massachusetts, at a place called Camp Kenwood. I had brought in my old trainer Hiawatha Grey along with a trainer from Toledo, James "Cheerful" Norman. Cheerful and Hiawatha were jealous of each other and the place was soon an armed camp. My good luck charm, Poppa Dee, a seventy-five-year-old medicine man, tub-thumper and camp handy man, arrived and seemed to pour coal on the fire. The sparring partners, Clint Bacon, Johnny Jenkins and Jesse "Gorilla" Brown, all seemed to have a great time. Not me. I was on long-distance with my friend.

I was ready to burst. Trying to be a peacemaker, trying to pacify her and trying to ballyhoo the fight had my nerves on a constant ragged edge. The publicity must have reflected my short temper, as I read that I was a swell-headed clown. One fool publicity man from the International Boxing Club even suggested I visit Brockton, Rocky's hometown, and slug Rocky's father! I'm not kidding. He actually suggested that.

However, publicity, favorable or unfavorable, does build the gate for a fight, and we drew the ninth largest gate in boxing history. When I stepped into the ring I was confronted by Harry Kessler, who had been assigned as referee. Why Charley Johnston didn't protest is a mystery to me. Here was the specter of my childhood, and the man who almost spoiled my unanimous win over Maxim. I felt I now had to fight two men. How right I was.

The first round was nothing. The fight had been postponed a day, due to the threat of hurricane *Ione*, and we were both edgy and cautious. In the second round I spotted an opening. Rocky lunged in with a wide right hand, and I pivoted away, then came back with a half right uppercut. Though I was too far out to get the best leverage, he dropped like a pound of mashed potatoes on a tile floor. I went to the farthest neutral corner. Kessler began counting. One, two, Rocky was up but Kessler went on, three, four. The mandatory count does not apply in championship bouts, but Kessler must have been excited, too. My seconds were screaming for me to finish him and I moved to do so, but Kessler got there ahead of me. He carefully wiped off Rocky's gloves, giving him another few seconds, and then when he released him he gave him a sort of stiff jerk, which may have helped Rocky clear his head. When Rocky first got back on his feet he had an elbow on the ropes and was staring out at the crowd. I know. I was there. I was so furious at Kessler I thought I'd better hit him first and get that obstacle out of the way. But as it was, I turned to fight Rocky and I was blind and stupid with rage. And my rage wasn't directed at Marciano, because so far he was the only one cooperating with me. I began to slug toe-to-toe with Rock. At that he didn't catch up with me until the ninth round when he fought me back into my own corner, and I was still trying to keep my shell defense effective. I caught a left hook to the body, and from habit I covered for an expected right hand, but he threw another left hook and that one caught me in the head. I saw it coming, but I was like a man in a trance. The punch knocked me down and he had me. I think a knockout is the only way to end a championship fight and I went out the way a good fighter should go, taking the full count.

I must say that the cheer that went up when I decked Marciano was the most thrilling and inspiring sound I have ever heard. You cannot imagine what the roar of 60,000 people can do to your spine. You stand under the lights with a fallen champion at your feet and, as one voice, the crowd salutes you. It is a thrill that cannot be measured, and it is a memory I can conjure up by just closing my eyes. I realize that when I was knocked out the same crowd saluted Rocky, and that's as it should be. In sports you have to face the fact that they cheer winners.

This fight was on September 21, 1955, and it was said that I was all washed up. They claimed no one was ever any good after the Rock had worked on them. In 1958, three years later, I won the Boxer of the Year award, and I guess my pal Rocky hadn't done such a good job after all.

When two fighters who respect each other have fought a hard, tough go, they usually develop a camaraderie that lasts forever. It is the feeling that they have shared something no other people have, and it is a binding tie. I feel this way about Rocky, and I hope he has a long and pleasant life doing what he wants to do when he wants to. I know many men in "civilian" life whose friendship began in a fight. It is one of the mysteries of human nature.

I went out night-clubbing after the fight. I had helped Lucky Thompson get a booking by promising to show up at the club, win, lose or draw, and so there I was. Lucky greeted me sourly. He was angry because he had bet some money on me and had lost. But even in the face of his surly and ungrateful behavior I felt fine. I felt I had done the best I could, although losing my temper wasn't the best ring strategy. And as the years go on, I'll become more and more convinced I lost to Kessler, not to Marciano.

My share of the purse for the Marciano fight was over $240,000. After the fight I went to business manager Reese and asked for my money, but he said it had to be held up until the tax figures were settled and the TV revenue checked. I didn't realize at the time that I would be stalled for a year. Now I was supposed to go to London to fight Yolande Pompey. Reese said that with the purses from Olson, Marciano and Pompey I'd be able to build the motel I had been thinking about. I replied that if I didn't have enough money right now, then I didn't want to build a motel. The estimate I had gotten for the structure was $65,000. He became angry and said if I didn't want to fight Pompey, he was through, as he had more important things to do. Actually, my end of the Olson fight was $89,000 and for Marciano I got $270,000, and I think I should have been able to build a motel so fancy they wouldn't let me check in. But I was off to England, so that was that.

I paid my lady friend about $12,000. One lump of $5,000 and then dribs and drabs of $200 and $300 payments. But I hadn't heard the end of it yet. I left for England, thinking or hoping it was behind me.

Charley Johnston flew to England with me. We stayed overnight in London and the next morning we went to Windsor, where Windsor Castle is. As I looked up at it, I thought if I had my money, here was a ready-made motel. We lived a block and a half from the castle at the Star and Garter Hotel. They told me the hotel was 500 years old, but it certainly was in good shape. It had a gymnasium on the second floor of the annex, and there was plenty of action around there when I started to train, for England has a great many amateur boxers, as it is still quite a gentleman's sport over there. I used to run in Windsor Park every morning, from the hotel into the park to the copper horse and then back. Cheerful Norman was my trainer, and I brought Clint Bacon along to spar with me. The cold weather affected my reducing system and I was having trouble making the weight. At the weigh-in, I was amused to see a bookmaker's blackboard set up, as the people would bet on anything. They reminded me of the Australians. They were making bets on the exact weight the scales would give Pompey and me.

The Pompey fight was pretty good. We had had a press party earlier and Pompey, naturally, said he was going to win. I amused the press by lecturing him on impatience, and I pointed out how many years I had waited and suggested he get set to wait a few years himself. He laughed and the press seemed to enjoy themselves, and I did later when I knocked Pompey out in the ninth round. Pompey has quit the ring, but he was a good opponent.

After the fight I visited Epsom Downs and wore my morning coat and striped trousers, ascot tie and pearl top hat. Ingemar Johansson had been at the fight, and a day or two later he was announced from the lobby. He was so excited he grabbed me by the collar and insisted we make a match on the spot and fight in his home town, Goteborg, Sweden. He assured me we could draw $60,000, but as I had just made $50,000 for myself this didn't seem too appealing. I explained to him that I had been signed to fight the Canadian heavyweight James J. Parker in six weeks, so a bout in Sweden would be impossible.

The promotion for the Parker fight stands out in my memory. To help build the gate I had a wide-awake press agent named Saul Richman, and among his other clients was the After Six formal wear company. Saul ballyhooed the fight as the return of the gentlemanly art, and arranged for the first ten rows ringside to be occupied only by people dressed formally. The sports writers got with it. It was good copy. They were all in dinner jackets and even Doc Kearns had on tails with black-and-white shoes to set him off dazzlingly. As a press stunt it was great, but poor Parker got kayoed in the ninth and some of the gentlemen of the press got blood spattered on their white evening jackets.

Marciano had retired from boxing and Patterson and I were named the logical contenders for succession to his throne. I began to train for the fight with Floyd, and my friend came back on the scene.

She began to harass me, asking for money, and at first I ignored her and then told her to see Reese. I don't know what came of that, but just before the Patterson fight she brought charges against me that I had beaten her up and molested her daughter. Her daughter was twelve years old, and why a woman would even want to have her daughter's name in such a case is unthinkable. The charge was ridiculous and disgusting, and my attorney had the case dismissed.

Later, this woman got into other trouble and went to jail.

During the time Reese was my business manager I not only paid the woman $12,000, which needn't have been paid if I had been advised to go to the police, but I also paid substantial legal and accounting fees. Recently I read how Reese was a great benefactor of mine. They must be talking about someone else. I also read he had given me a job for $75 a week. I deny this. Any money he advanced me he was mighty sure to get back. I'm a great one for understatement.

I had to live with the nightmare for some time. I have told my wife Joan the whole story, leaving nothing out, and she understands. It happened before I ever met her, and never would have happened had I met Joan before I played that theater in Cleveland.

But that visit backstage was the long arm of worry that reached out and tapped me before I got into the ring with Patterson. My practice of relaxism was sorely neglected that night. He finally helped me to relax.

# ROUND 10 DOWN BUT NOT OUT

I trained hard for the Patterson fight—too hard. I overtrained. I was stale, I was worried, and I was beaten as badly as I have ever been beaten in my whole ring career. But it was on the level. Floyd Patterson won, and that is that.

I didn't expect to get raves after the fight but I was surprised when the writers took me apart the way they did. I've always conceded they are entitled to their opinions and I seldom have disputes with anything written about me, but I must protest strongly when it is hinted I dumped the fight. To do so I would have had to have a reason, and the only reason would be that I had bet money on Floyd. It takes a minimum of two to make a bet, and if the man I bet with will come forward I'll be glad to meet him for the first time. If I had won the fight, I would have been the holder of the heavy and light heavyweight titles. I think it would have meant quite a few dollars in the Moore bank account. The odds weren't favorable for a "killing," and when you rule money out there isn't another reason for me to go into the tank. After all, my share of that fight was $118,300.50. Even with my troubles, with the Marciano purse I wasn't hurtin'.

Floyd Patterson is a gentleman. He is honest and good. He can fight. I would like to fight him again. At this writing he is scheduled to fight the champion Ingemar Johansson in a return match. I would like to fight the winner. I think I can beat either one of them.

Johansson has a strong right hand. We all know that now. Yvon Durelle had a strong right hand. He proved it in his first fight with me, but in our second fight I made a point of avoiding his right. I think I can avoid Johansson's right hand, too. I have always been able to hit an opponent, and it would be interesting to see how Ingo reacts to being hit. The only fighter worth anything that he has fought besides Patterson is Eddie Machen, and Machen is a very cautious fighter. I'm not saying Machen doesn't have guts but he fights a highly conservative fight. Johansson, in my opinion, hasn't been pressed as yet. Maybe Patterson will push him this time and maybe not, but I'm ready and waiting to throw a few right hands at the winner, no matter who it is.

Patterson didn't surprise me when we fought. I knew what type of fight to expect and I got it. I planned to bring the fight to him and I wasn't able to. My reflexes were off and my timing was terrible. I couldn't put together any combinations. I like to work a left jab, a right-hand feint and then a hard left hook to the body to rock an opponent. I believe a strong hook to the body can do more lasting damage than a shot to the jaw. If you can hit a man high on the rib cage with a lot of strength behind it, you can hamper the movements of his arm on whatever side you hit him. And, knowing this, you can work on that side with comparative freedom. It affects the arm much more than a direct punch on the arm. A fighter's arms are his defensive armor. Why waste punches on armor? You can only develop a certain amount of toughness on the stomach and upper part of the body. A good punch will get through.

A good jab is a necessity to a fighter. It is the first punch taught to aspiring boxers. If a boy can learn a jab and jab well you can teach him other things. But if he can't master the jab he's finished then and there. A jab is a punch designed for maneuvering or putting an opponent off balance. I can jab and pivot on my left foot in a complete circle, making my opponent take three steps to my one as he circles to keep me in front of him. But a jab alone seldom wins a fight. When I broke my hand against the Australian champion Richards, I literally jabbed him to death, but it was a move made in desperation and it is not recommended as an aggressive weapon. However, if you have damaged a man's face with a previous punch, the jab can effectively pester him and add to the hurt you have already inflicted. Ray Robinson is a master at using his jab to follow up an advantage. Patterson has a good jab and I think that I have one, too. But body-punching is what wins fights. I know it looks great to see a boxer hit a man on the jaw and knock him down, but usually a few good body punches have softened him up. The real hard hitters like Dempsey and Louis could certainly belt a man in the kisser and cool him, but most fighters rely on a little more preparation.

It is disheartening, indeed, to put all you have in one punch and then find the man still there in front of you. Believe me when I say that night against Patterson I wanted to grab hold of the ring stool and flatten him. I just couldn't get through to him, and I'm quite sure if I had been lucky and connected solidly I wouldn't have been able to finish him. It just wasn't my night.

Sometimes you take that long walk from the dressing room to the ring and along the way your high spirits fade. Call it lethargy, call it a fit of depression, but it enervates and knocks off your efficiency. Prior to the fight, I felt well physically and had temporarily shelved my worries about the lawsuit pending against me, yet by the time I climbed through the ropes I had had it. It all seemed strange, almost as though I was a spectator and not one of the participants.

Don't take this as an alibi. It is an explanation. So much has been written about the fight that I want to give you my feelings. I openly admit I was beaten fairly by a good fighter. It is no shame to be beaten by the Heavyweight Champion of the World. It's always better to win, but if you won 'em all you'd become a dull fighter. I'm in my twenty-fifth year (give or take a couple) of prize fighting and I've lost many fights, but never did I lose one in such sorry fashion as the night I fought Floyd Patterson. My handlers were amazed. So, evidently, was everybody else. I was favored to win, but I was a far cry from being cocky as I sat waiting for the first bell.

People often ask me how fighters can stand the pain of being punched constantly, especially in cases like Carmen Basilio the night Sugar Ray tagged his eye and kept hitting it time after time. It is quite true that if you were standing on a street corner and Ray Robinson spun you around and belted you in the eye, the pain would be unbearable. But I have found that in the ring the excitement and the tenseness of the situation causes the level of pain to lower. By that I mean the adrenalin seems to insulate you against sharp pain. You always feel the first punch, but, quite naturally, since you are in a fight you assume there will be some punching going on. After the first bodily contact is made, you seem to grow more or less numb and you concentrate on your own hitting. Often, between rounds, the pain of a punch comes through, but it disappears again when the bell rings and you concentrate on the business at hand. I have been hit terrific blows, and knew when I was hit that they were terrific, and yet the pain really didn't begin to bother me until I was back in the dressing room. In my last Durelle fight, just before I finished him, he threw his best punch of the fight, a hard right hand over my heart. A paralyzing body punch. It hurt and I knew he had landed, but he didn't realize it. Luckily, it didn't impair my left and the fight was over seconds later.

Floyd Patterson hurt me. I felt it and knew immediately I was off. Whenever I can feel punches acutely, I know there is something wrong with me. Obviously my mental responses were not normal, or his punches would have been like any others. But I hadn't felt excitement or tension and the pain was there. After all, he is by no means the hardest puncher I have fought. Marciano can deal you a clout to remember, but in my fight with him, although I was battered and bruised, I can honestly say I felt less pain in the ring with him than I did with Floyd.

I hope to get another shot at the heavyweight title. And if I do, I'm confident the decision will go my way. I'm maturing as a fighter, and I want to restore the confidence the press had in me. It was most gratifying to read sports writers all over the country when they registered indignation over the N.B.A. ruling that relieved me of the light heavyweight title. I thought it was unjust and the matter was rectified shortly after, but that display of confidence in me was what counted most. Commissioner Maceroni, by the way, didn't make that decision on his own. The council of N.B.A. voted on the ruling and he put it into force. When the title was restored, he again announced the decision. I bear no malice. It was wonderful publicity for a kid trying to get along in the boxing game.

After the Patterson fight, I resumed my career as light heavyweight champion. Of course, I took a vacation in between, as I wasn't too pressed for money. Finally, Kearns and Johnston told me to get ready, for they had arranged matches in Germany for me. I was supposed to have gone to Germany after the Pompey fight, but something happened and I had to return to America for the Parker fight in Toronto. I had been looking forward to visiting Germany, and I eagerly began training for the trip and the fights that would result. I had truly become a global fighter, having had bouts from Tasmania to Stuttgart, from Toronto to the Argentine.

I took Lucky Thompson with me. I bought him a new saxophone and I taught him how to be my second, and he worked in my corner in both fights in Germany. Lucky is still in Europe as I write this, but he and I drifted apart. We boarded a plane in San Diego for the first leg of the long flight to Germany.

I found Germany to be a very fine place and was amazed at the atmosphere of industry everywhere. I could hardly believe the positive evidences of recovery I saw at every turn, as Essen had been completely leveled during the war. All new buildings, new streets and a real air of hustle around, as the people scurried down the avenues. I was extremely sorry I was in training, as we visited many fine restaurants and the culinary odors were driving me out of my mind. The Germans became boxing conscious after the great success of Max Schmeling when he beat Joe Louis. His subsequent defeat didn't dampen their ardor, for they naturally thought the Americans had purposely arranged the fight to give a Negro a victory over a pure Aryan. The fact that Schmeling won his fight fairly and then lost most decisively had no bearing on the matter. But by the time I got there the attitude towards Negroes was all sweetness and light. They treated me as a champion and as a welcome visitor. And, in my opinion, with all politics aside, I think Schmeling was the best fighter Germany ever produced.

On May 1, 1957, I fought Hans Kalbfell in Essen. It went to ten rounds and I won the decision. On June 2 I fought the Belgian champion, Alain Cherville, in Stuttgart and I knocked him out in the sixth round. Now I was ready to go to Paris with Lucky and dig the jazz scene I'd read and heard so much about. But even as my ears were watering, thinking of that cool music, word came that I would have to return immediately to the United States.

A hassle arose over my not fighting Tony Anthony. They were threatening to relieve me of the title if I didn't fight him. You see, before I left the States Doc Kearns had made arrangements for me to fight Chuck Spizer. Well, Spizer chose to fight Anthony instead. His manager must have booked the Anthony fight as a warm-up for the match against me. But to Anthony it was no warm-up. He knocked Spizer out in three rounds. There was a forfeit of $15,000, which Doc said would have to be gotten in court, but as yet I haven't seen any of the money, nor have I been inside a court on the matter. So I demanded a $100,000 guarantee to fight Anthony. It was finally settled at $90,000 if I won.

While I was in training, I asked to have the fight postponed a month because my wife Joan was going to have a baby. I was afraid the excitement would be bad for her, and I was having trouble concentrating on my work myself. The promoter said that Joan was having the baby not me, and the fight went on as scheduled.

This boy was young enough to be my son, and that fact plus the $90,000 made me punch from bell to bell right through the fight. I kept the pressure on him and finally kayoed him in the seventh round, and several days later Joan gave birth to our daughter Rena.

I had three more fights that year and won them all, two by knockouts. Late in 1957 I returned to South America, more a hero than ever, and I enjoyed the trip immensely. People still frown on my obvious love for South America, but there is absolutely no color barrier there and most white people simply cannot appreciate how I felt, moving freely wherever I wanted. My love for South America is almost idealistic, since the attitude down there is what I would love to experience in North America at some future time. It's like having a beautiful wife you love who is cold to you, and then finding a plain mistress who adores you. The United States is my home and I love it dearly, but every once in a while I wink slyly at South America and she winks back.

After two fights in South America, I returned and had seven more fights before returning to San Diego to train for my first fight with Yvon Durelle. That fight is significant to me, for it gave me the world's record of the most number of knockouts—127 (now 128)—and the fight was so sensational I was named Fighter of the Year.

# ROUND 11 THE SALT MINE

I think that I am the only active fighter who owns his own training camp. I'm sure I'm the only one who owns two. One is a small ranch called the Whistle Stop, near my San Diego home where I train boys for local amateur tournaments, and the other is a large ranch outfitted solely to condition and train professional fighters. I named it the Salt Mine, and it is located about 37 miles northwest of San Diego at the foot of Mount Woodson, near the town of Ramona. One hundred twenty acres of rugged terrain spread out in the most wonderful climate in the world. My privacy is sometimes invaded by rattlesnakes and an occasional curious mountain lion, but since shooting is one of my hobbies these visitors heighten my interest in my ranch. I have a long-range improvement plan in work at the Salt Mine against the day I retire from the ring. At that time I would like to open a health camp for harried business men and keep up the training facilities for use by West Coast fighters.

On the property I have five houses with an average of five rooms each, kitchen facilities and equipment for year-round living; two swimming pools, one of which I am going to convert into a unique bar, as I intend to build a much larger central swimming pool. I have an outdoor gym and an indoor gym. Both gyms have a regulation boxing ring, complete with raised apron, for I also teach budding fight managers how to work as seconds for their amateur tigers. Around the borders of my "estate" I have a natural roadwork trail with complete circuits of 4, 6 and 7 miles. The roadwork is done uphill and down, with several good flat stretches. Walking up hill backwards is a great way to build the muscles of the calves. I have bulldozed 8 miles of twisting and climbing roads on my land, and perhaps someday in the far off future I will have them paved. Right now they are oil-treated, and it lends an air of roughing it to sports writers who visit me. Currently I am building a dam with the aid of the State of California, which will give me a lake of 12 acres and will be stocked with fish. I will build tennis courts and a pitch-and-putt golf course to round out the recreational advantages I can offer to my future clients. I will also have whirlpool baths, steam rooms and rubbing tables and my plans include a laundry on the premises, a large dining room and social hall. I'd like to do that kind of work and I think I've gained the know-how through the years. The place will feature my diet, and getting rid of excess pounds may be the main attraction.

In the first Durelle fight I was knocked down three times in the first round, and everyone thought Yvon was the new champion. But after managing to survive, I got him in the eleventh and referee Jack Sharkey raised my hand in victory. It was said to be the toughest fight of my career, and I was justifiably proud of having done the impossible. The fight was in December, and I was invited to many, many banquets and the old appetite was in there swinging, and I plumped up very fast. The day the rematch with Durelle was set I took stock of my physical condition and I knew the hardest fight was going to be the fight to make the weight. I called my old friend and trainer Hiawatha Grey and asked him to leave his home in Indianapolis and join me at camp. He is a ring general, a student of strategy and the man who tells me if my punch is on or off. Soon after Hi arrived I sent to Oakland for my other trainer, Dick Saddler. It is his responsibility to get me into the best possible shape, and it is almost split-second timing. Training a prize fighter is much like training a race horse. The thoroughbred must be brought to a peak condition on a certain day at a certain time to give the best performance. A fighter is exactly the same. Overtraining can be fatal, just as over-confidence or "dogging it" can be.

My average day in training is about like this: I wake up at six or seven, no set time, and judge the weather. It happens quite rarely, but once in a while a very wet, dense fog settles in the mountains and I wait until the sun cuts through before I go on my road stint. My main objective is to perspire and lose weight while I'm strengthening my legs, and a damp fog would be detrimental to this aim. I may or may not have a cup of black coffee before I run and I sometimes take a jigger of blackberry wine for energy. I run between 4 and 7 miles and again I judge this for myself. My quarters are separate from my staff and they can sleep later, as I get into action in the morning on my own. Dieting makes a person irritable. I have enough contact with the boys during the day, so I don't hang around to bug them at night when they want to relax themselves. I don't mean I get nasty, but I am touchy and little things bother me. My sparring partner and, every so often, a brave visitor run with me. But before he gets to camp, in the early days of training, I run alone. Back in camp, I eat breakfast still dressed in my road togs. These, by the way, consist of flannel pants, sweatshirt and a coverall such as mechanics wear. Heavy running shoes and a towel draped around my head complete the outfit. My breakfast is usually a half melon and coffee (black), with an occasional poached egg from time to time. Then I am put to bed by Sadler and Grey and these fiends spoon-feed me two hot cups of tea while I'm wrapped and helpless in the blankets. To a man perspiring all this is as welcome as a high wave on a life raft.

One day a reporter asked to go along for roadwork with me and Junius Washington, my sparring partner. Now, I carry a.45 revolver in case I see a snake and also an army surplus canteen to rinse my mouth of dust. The reporter eyed the revolver and finally couldn't resist asking why I carried it. Before I could think of a reason Junius glumly said, "He's got that to keep me away from the canteen."

After my high tea I'm supposed to sleep, but as soon as the trainers leave I put on my tape machine and play jazz as I dose. Jazz is my palliative. My minor irritations go away and I can relax. I have hundreds of spools of tapes. Jazz of all kinds, and much of it recorded by me on the spot. To anyone on a diet I strongly recommend some outside interest. A person with a hobby has it made, but other people have to find something to take their minds off the constant gnawing pangs of hunger. I have found music my greatest asset when I'm in training. It relaxes me as much as body massage. I sleep for two or two and a half hours and then I go into a hot tub where I soak for half an hour. Next Saddler gives me a brisk rub, and Hiawatha fixes me a glass of plain gelatin dissolved in a half glass of water. I take that for instant energy, for now I'm ready for my afternoon workout. I'm outlining this average day so you will realize a fighter earns his money long before he steps into the ring for a few rounds of dancing. Everyone seems to think that for an evening measured in minutes a man gets an awful lot of money. It just isn't so. When you read of Archie Moore getting a seventy-five-or hundred-thousand-dollar guarantee it seems like a bonanza. But by now you realize that the days of eating on 75 cents are just paying off.

During the early days of training my workouts are held in the indoor gym. This is a veritable sweatbox. It is a converted barn and the heat is fierce. Junius and I get into the ring and shadow-box for two three-minute rounds. This limbers us up and gives us our "fighting breath." Learning to breathe properly is part of prize fighting. With a mouthpiece on in a tough fight you have to know how and when to gulp in some air. We take a normal minute rest between shadow-boxing rounds. Then we box each other for two rounds, and Junius works on whatever Hiawatha has told him to. For instance, he may be told to throw right crosses so I can practice slipping a hook inside. The hook deflects the right-hand shot and changes from a defense parry to an aggressive thrust. Junius Washington is from Oakland, California, and he is managed by my trainer Dick Saddler and I think he's a fine fighter.

After the boxing I do two rounds on the speed bag. That's the little bag you always see in the movies when the gangster enters the gym and waves his cigar at the fight manager. The manager tells his boy to work out on the light bag. The rat-a-tat-tatting of the bag is the background noise as the gangster tells the manager his boy has to throw the fight. Actually it's used to sharpen your eye and give snap to your jabs.

From the speed bag I move to the heavy bag. Now, this bag plays a different part in pictures. The heavy sandbag is usually hugged by someone to give it stability when you practice hooks and crosses. In movies it is held by a former champ who is down on his luck, and between grunts he says to the fighter, "I know they asked you to dump the Martinelli fight, Champ, but don't do it. They'll just use you and throw you away. I know." The Champ, feeling guilty because he's already got the money spent, merely scowls and hits the bag even harder.

Next I skip rope for two rounds. This is more conditioning for my legs. Skipping rope helps your balance and tones the muscles you have built in roadwork. Surely you know where rope-skipping fits in fight films? Why, that's when the gangster's pretty playmate appears. She's a blonde with the right curves and as we see her she is watching the Champ skip rope. She tells the gangster that she's been missing a lot through the years, and he worries his cigar a bit and tells her to go out and wait in the car. But she and the Champ have exchanged winks by now. The scene ends with a close-up of the manager, who has seen and understands the danger.

But at the Salt Mine there are no movie cameras grinding. Just old Archie grinding away fat. Any pretty girl who came out and asked about me might very well be answered by my beautiful wife Joan, who has a left hook equal to my own. My wife often visits camp in the afternoon with my two adorable daughters, Rena and Joan, and I have an hour or so before dinner to relax with them.

Dinner is my time for fun. Any friends who have dropped by to watch me work are invited to stay. We cook steaks on the barbecue grill and tell jokes and talk fighting until the coffee is all gone and the sherbet is in my belly where it belongs. I am a frozen-sherbet fanatic and have challenged all flavors.

Now a few words about the boys who help me with my training. Dick Saddler is a natural comedian, a man with great heart and a sagacious adviser. To be with the same men all day for weeks on end can be a strain, but Dick manages to relieve this with his spontaneous humor and logic. He is a former fighter and I couldn't have anyone better in my corner when I'm fighting. I can knock more than wood that I have not been seriously injured during a fight, but the fact that Dick is there makes a big difference to me. He is an expert at split-second first aid, which can often mean pulling a fight out of the fire. Dick is my friend, a churchman, a good citizen.

Hiawatha Grey is a wise old owl. He don't say "Who?," he say "When?" He can figure opponents better than anyone I've ever met. His overall strategy for the second Durelle fight was a masterpiece. He has more dignity than Elsa Maxwell at a Perle Mesta party. It would be wise to be married to him for fourteen years before calling him Hiawatha. He goes his own way. I have had a key to his front door for more than twenty years and there is a bed and food waiting for me should I ever need it. Need I say more?

Junius Washington, my sparring partner, is a young man with quick reflexes, a hard jab and a taste for life. He is quiet and doesn't speak unless he has something definite to say, and as a road companion he is ideal. Part of our roadwork tour passes through a farmyard and a particularly vicious spaniel lived there. I don't believe this dog was civilized. He would rush out and snap at Junius and myself every morning. It tended to help me reduce, because I would pick Junius up in my arms and race away like 'Liza crossing the ice with that dog snap ping and snarling behind me. One day I decided I had had enough. I made up my mind to shoot the dog. "Don't do it," said Junius. "He'll buy another dog and it might be bigger."

When I'm involved getting ready for a fight there are many things that have to be done that I haven't the time for. Letters to be written, phone calls, appointments, etc. I've found I need a Jack of all trades: secretary, assistant, official greeter, host, and so on. The Jack I use is really a Jill; for my wife, Joan, takes care of all these things for me.

She also helps me and Doc bargain for fight purses and television guarantees, and she helps my accountant work out my income tax. Come to think of it, I don't know how I got along without her all these years.

At the camp we pretty much do for ourselves. We make our own beds, do daily laundry in our washing machines, cook, wash floors and do our own dishes. I must say, in all honesty, that except for making my bed and helping with the Saturday morning mopping, I have few other domestic chores, as I am usually engaged in some phase of physical training. No one tells anyone else what to do, but anyone who shirks soon hears about it from the other fellows. I do not allow hard liquor on the premises, nor pin-up pictures, but I keep some beer on ice for visitors and the boys for a Saturday night two-can spree. In the evenings the boys play cards and watch television. They are free to drive into San Diego, if they wish. We have many pick-up trucks at the ranch, and Hiawatha always has his car. In my own cabin, I put on music tape and read and answer personal mail. I write to people all over the world. I have been writing to sports writers for many years. They have often complimented me by reprinting my letters. I firmly believe publicity is a great thing, if you have something to sell. I also think it is good for the fight game in general, if it is favorable, for it stimulates public interest and helps build a better gate. My manager, steeped in wisdom, the venerable Jack 'Doc' Kearns, made up this old maxim (not Joey) that says: the more people who attend a fight, the bigger the gate.

I think boxing today is slowly getting better. The public has gotten wise to "behind-the-scenes" managers and is making the various commissions do something about it. To me boxing, like the legitimate theater, is a fabulous invalid. The game will always have sharpies and illegitimate operators nosing around. But let's keep them on the fringes, and that's the best you can do.

One of the big kicks I get at the Salt Mine is watching fights on TV. The two trainers, Dick and Hiawatha, bet nickels, each picking a corner to bet on for the evening. Then when the fight starts each trainer screams advice or admonishes his "boy," who may be fighting three thousand miles away. Their rage and frustration sends me into gales of laughter.

The Salt Mine, like most ranches, has an assortment of pets. I have two dogs, a hen and a rooster, a cat and assorted snakes. The two dogs are father and son, the hen and rooster are man and wife. The snakes are dead as soon as I see them. The snake problem, by the way, lessens each year. As the ranch grows more populated and traffic increases, the wild life that the snakes feed on leaves, taking their rattle-shaking enemies with them. The nuisance of snakes is not so much the fear of being bitten, for they won't attack unless cornered or stepped on, and we wear high shoes at all times. The nuisance is that when you kill a snake that is poisonous you must cut off the head and bury it so no domestic animal has an opportunity to swallow it.

My hen is a character. She made her roost on top of the platform supporting the speed bag, and during a workout sits calmly up there as the whole world crashes and bangs around her. After Junius and I have given that bag twelve minutes of pounding, I don't know why she doesn't lay scrambled eggs. Trying to dislodge the hen has sharpened my jabs no end, and I advise Harold John son to buy himself a good settin' hen right away.

The expenses of a training camp are many and varied. Besides the main expenditure on food and staples, we have daily equipment costs. We use about $2 worth of bandages every day to tape our hands. (Advice to young beginners: buy heavy gauze bandage that can be washed and used over and over again.) Two pair of boxing shoes are required. One pair is broken in and put aside for the fight, the other pair gets worn out during training. The sparring partner has the same requirements, for he usually fights a preliminary fight on the same card. Roadwork shoes get hard usage, and two pairs usually suffice for the training period. Replacement of gym equipment isn't a steady or fixed item, but things are constantly wearing out or in need of repair. The outdoor ring has two canvas sides hung against prevailing winds, and this year I have to build a small grandstand for spectators. We have, thank goodness, a steady flow of people from the press, radio and TV, and some entertainment costs for these welcome guests must be met. I have open house at my camp and, although I can't feed everyone who drops by, no charge is made to watch the daily workouts and children are most welcome. After my years of sweaty gyms, tough-talking fight fans and hours spent killing time in pool rooms, I now appreciate children. They are honest and eager, and their admiration of a man who owns the title of champion is sincere and unaffected, and most enjoyable.

Maintenance costs continue. Gasoline, electricity and an awful amount of soap. Mail and publicity expenses, travel and payroll for the staff. Over a period of nine weeks this can add up to quite an amount, and that is why training camp costs are always figured in when I sign to fight for my title. Usually the last ten days or two weeks of training are done away from the Salt Mine and near the scene of battle. For the second Durelle fight I went to Montreal.

Two days before leaving California for Montreal, I came in from roadwork and had a terrible blister on my heel. A friend, Bob Condon, had been running with me, and the two of us said nothing to my trainers, for I knew they would put me to bed. I wanted to go to Los Angeles the following day for a conference with Sam Goldwyn, Jr., concerning the possibility of my playing the role of Jim the slave in a film version of Mark Twain's classic *Huckleberry Finn*. I went up as scheduled with a bandage on the heel, but a day in street shoes was no help at all. When I returned I revealed the condition to the trainers but we all decided we'd best leave for Montreal, for a postponement from California would raise serious doubts and could kill any appeal the fight might have. We had three weeks ahead of us to ballyhoo the attraction, and we all believed the heel would come round with care and attention. We stopped in New York to see the Patterson-Johansson fight, but it was postponed so we flew to Montreal and I watched it on television. Johansson won, by the way.

# ROUND 12 THE BIG FISHERMAN

In December, 1958, I had fought Yvon Durelle, a husky, game fisherman who had earned a good name in Canadian boxing. I was knocked down three times in the first round and again in the fifth but came back to win by a knockout in the eleventh. It was my finest hour. I was Fighter of the Year, and won the Edward J. Neil trophy given by the Boxing Writer's Association. The fight also gave me the world's record for the most knockouts, passing by one Young Stribling's long-standing record of 126. This is a record I doubt will ever be broken, as the pattern of the fight game is changed. The small clubs are gone and fighters without proper seasoning are shoved in front of TV cameras. The careers of fighters will be shortened, and it takes a few years and many many fights to score a hundred or more knockouts.

Many people have asked me about that first Durelle fight. It puzzled students of boxing to see a seasoned veteran get caught off guard in the first round and almost lose the fight. A lot of things happened to cause that and most of them were hard right-hand shots. The Forum in Montreal is the home of hockey, and consequently it is a bit chilly in the winter months. The boards for the floor, seats and ring, are laid over ice. It was three degrees in my corner as I sat and waited for the bell. For a San Diego boy this can be troublesome. I was stiff; I need to be loose and limber. Durelle helped me in that. Being bounced on your back may be a poor way to burp the baby, but all it did for me was loosen me up and make me realize that fighting from a supine position is difficult at best. I recall saying to myself that I wanted to hurry back to the hotel and rejoin my wife. Our baby, 'Rene, had said goodbye to me while leaping up and down on the bed. She was wearing bright red pajamas and had said her daddy was going to make boom-boom, which was her way of describing prize fighting. Durelle made boom-boom, and the next time I thought of 'Rene was when I was on the canvas taking another count from able referee Jack Sharkey.

Much of the fun in winning fights is not losing. This well-thought-out philosophy stuck in my mind after the bell sounded ending the first round. I frankly couldn't believe what was going on. Doc Kearns, ever fearless, told me not to worry. Relaxism was the key word. I believed everything even less in the fifth round when he floored me again. I had gone into my shell and practiced escapology, but in the fifth he exploded again. From the sixth round on I was in charge. Durelle is not a finisher. Once I knew that for sure, I could plan my fight and I did. I went on to score an amazing win and, through my blush of modesty, may I say no man deserved it more. But Durelle proved to be a tough puncher, a young man with a lot of guts and damn near World's Light Heavyweight Champion.

My trainers and I had this in mind when we sat down for a strategy meeting at the Salt Mine. We decided my best bet was to rush Durelle and force him to make a mistake, counting on my obvious superior experience to make him "go" clumsy. Now that I was fully aware of his dangerous right hand I could fend it off. I didn't fear his left and still don't, but I did respect his right. I also have a great deal of respect for my own right, since it has been putting cool sherbet in my mouth for some time. And I knew that a split-second opportunity was all I needed. I am known to have a vicious hook that can set a man up for a knockout and I was willing to use it. This, then, was what we had decided in California, but a man named Charley Goldman changed all that for us.

Meanwhile my heel got more and more aggravated. I was favoring the foot. A fighter must have two able feet as well as his hands. Even today Jack Dempsey could give you a hit you wouldn't want, but what stopped him from fighting was the lasting legs needed for a title bout. Your balance, your moving in and out, spinning and just standing up for fifteen rounds all depends on the conditioning you give your legs and how they respond when you need them. With a bad foot I was under a severe handicap. I asked for a postponement, which is quite permissible in a championship fight. After all, why should the public pay for a fight that isn't all there? The date was moved up and I set out to heal the foot and nothing else. My weight, at that time, was 179 and making 175 was a snap. Once I get under 180 I've got it made. Most papers, of course, assumed I was having trouble making the weight and considered the bad heel a red herring.

The next postponement came when I got the terrible news that my wife had been rushed to the hospital for an emergency operation. I'm sure everyone understands the need for me to have gone to her. Here I must say Durelle was a true gentleman. In the words of Jacobs' Beach, he had a legitimate beef. There was the fear on his part of overtraining.

When my wife was out of danger, I returned and a new date was set. Hiawatha called another "board" meeting. Our strategy had to be changed. Charley Goldman entered the picture as Durelle's trainer. Hiawatha was convinced that Durelle was a puncher and could never be made a boxer. Not even the great Goldman could change that. Especially in the time he had. Believe me when I say all members of my camp have great respect for Charley Goldman. After all, he did train and refine Rocky Marciano, who had a bit of a go with me. But Hiawatha reasoned that Goldman would work on Durelle's style. Trying to think as Goldman would, Hiawatha believed Durelle would rush me and would be fighting in a sort of crouch. The way to circumvent any advantage a crouch might give him was to fight him head-on. Never let Durelle get on either side of me. I listened, we talked and finally we were all agreed. We had a pattern of battle mapped out, calling for a third-round knockout.

The first round was a minuet and we danced and got to know each other. But in the second round our strategy was entirely different. I would take a good left, the punch I didn't fear, and then go into my famous turtle shell defense—forearms blocking my chest, my hands in front of my face, posture slightly forward protecting my stomach, and the only target as I played peek-a-boo was the top of my head. As long as I kept him directly in front of me his hooks were ineffective. I did this. The result was exactly what we had planned. Hiawatha pointed out that the people of Montreal had bet heavily on their favorite son, counting on my old age against his youth and his showing against me the first time out. As soon as this audience saw him apparently beating me with punch after punch, they would begin to yell and scream in mounting crescendo. This is because fighting takes more than just being a witness to understand, and a lot of those people would be watching their first fight in the flesh. This yelling for Durelle would also have a telling effect on him. Now he of all people knew he really wasn't getting to me, but at the same time he was belting me and I wasn't belting back. Perhaps, he would think, the old boy is hurt. So he reverted to form and became a stand-up, free-swinging slugger and flailed away. My trainers were watching for this, as we had been waiting for the break away from Goldman's instructions, and they yelled the word. I dropped my hands and whipped out with a solid left hook. He was naturally exhausted by his own efforts and took the punch badly, and I knew I had him. He did catch me with one tremendous punch before the round was over and I was staggered. He hit me with a right hand over the heart and it really jolted me. He got me once in the third round with the same punch. But I was able to cover up, and the second round ended with Durelle right where I wanted him.

The third round was when we had planned to take him out. It was a question of his durability. The man has guts. He took plenty of hard punches. But I was finishing now. I threw plenty of assorted punches, missing some but landing more, swarming all over him. Jack Sharkey, the referee in both fights, had to let Durelle take the punishment. After all, in the first fight I was down three times and he didn't stop the fight, so he had to give Durelle the same consideration. I was a bit amused at the crowd, who, moments before, had been cheering wildly and were now staring in silent misbelief as I pounded their man to the canvas time after time. When he finally went down and it was obvious it was all over, they did give me an ovation, and I loved the Canadians all over again.

Now it sounds as though our battle strategy is easy to figure out after a fight and write down, but I have some proof and with your indulgence I'd like to give it to you. A good friend of mine, Bob Condon, a writer by trade, stayed at the training camp with me prior to the fight. We came East together and he was in Montreal the day of the fight. One day in New York Bob dropped in to his favorite haunt, the Absinthe House, and told his pals to bet on Dr. Moore. He picked me to win in the third round. His friends were slightly dubious, but one of his listeners was Charley Morey, the sports editor of the Associated Press Radio Sports Desk, and the following is what he sent over the AP wire on August 18, 1959. Take it, Mr. Morey.

*So you think this guy, Archie Moore, is an amazing guy? Well, you don't know the half of it. There's a true son of Broadway in New York named Bob Condon, a writer and close friend of Moore. Recently he went to San Diego to spend time with Archie.*

*He literally trained with Archie. He lived at Archie's training camp in the mountains, did road work with him, ate all his meals with him and got to know Archie quite well.*

*A few weeks ago Condon returned to New York. He told all his friends, "Moore will knock out Durelle in the third round." A few eyebrows were raised.*

*Condon replied, "I'm not kidding. Archie has a battle plan. He knows exactly what he will do in round one, round two and how he will finish off Durelle in round three. He explained it to me punch by punch."*

*You know what happened. Moore by a knockout in three rounds. At that old Arch drew it a little fine. The end came after 2 minutes and 52 seconds of the third. If the round had lasted 8 seconds more Archie would have been a failure as a prophet.*

But it didn't, Mr. Morey, and I later heard Bob's friends at the Absinthe House liked the odds so much they all bet on Durelle. But Bob was at ringside when I made his words as good as gold.

I finally got to the dressing room after the usual pandemonium in the ring. (I had asked my wife to come into the ring and accept the congratulations of the crowd.) Joan had been given permission to come East, and with her was her doctor, Dr. Kenneth Cales, and his wife. In the dressing room I was surrounded by my friends, well-wishers and some amazed Canadians. My two sparring partners (I added another for the Montreal training period) had each beaten a Durelle sparring partner on the same card. It was Moore and more of the same.

The jubilance continued. Can you recall the last day of school when you've been told you've been promoted and the whole glorious, carefree summer stretches ahead of you? That's how I feel after winning a big fight.

My wife and I were interviewed on tape recorders for later radio broadcasts to the States. My trainers posed for pictures, and even Poppa Dee had his picture taken. I like to have old Poppa Dee in my corner when I can. He's a talisman for me. He went to Australia many years ago to be a second for Li'l Arthur, who was, of course, the great heavyweight champion Jack Johnson. Poppa Dee has learned a little about boxing through the years.

The owner of the Chez Paree, a popular night club in Montreal, came into the dressing room and invited me and my friends as his guests for a victory celebration at his club. This is a part of championship fighting, too, that you've all seen in the movies. The winner has a ball while a consolation "wake" is held for the loser. I've had both kinds and I must say the victory kind is much the better. I felt like a hog in a corn bin and couldn't get the smile off my face. Now, the owner of the Chez Paree must have had more guts than

Durelle and I put together, as I had gathered up a small party of forty-seven by the time we were all seated. Certainly, I knew some of them!

Prior to going to the night club, I returned to the Croydon Hotel, which had been my headquarters. I had promised to call a couple of sports writers in San Diego and I also wanted a few quiet minutes to count my blessings and calm myself. Three or four of us sat quietly and we went over the fight again. Our strategy and my two hands had paid off and, frankly, we were all happily smug about it. Having used the audience as a psychological weapon tickled us most, for those in the audience who were pro-Durelle helped to beat him. I took inventory of my injuries. I could still feel exactly where Durelle had landed that body punch. The only other injury I could find was a bruised knuckle.

Dave Gregg, sports editor of the Joplin *Sun-Times* and a long-time close friend of mine, came in and broke up our session, and it was time to go to the party. Father Joe de Christina, my close friend and a Catholic priest, was with us, and I had a moment of apprehension when I thought of taking him to a night club. But his dignity was never assailed and it worked out just fine. He's Catholic and I'm a Baptist, but it never hurts to hedge your bet a little. Other pals from California were there and one, a comic named Redd Fox, had had his head shaved the day before so that only a monogram of "M" remained. The newspaper boys had taken pictures of his head, and it was quite funny and good publicity for both of us. Redd entertained at the party as did another pal of mine, a wonderful dancer named Foster Johnson.

The Canadians had never heard anything like Redd Fox before. Then there was a table of my sparring partners and their escorts, the trainers, the Forum officials, my press agent, Saul Richman and many, many others. I was the last to arrive, and again enjoyed on ovation as the people in the club recognized me. I was introduced from the night club floor and the party was on. I had a triple sherbet and the Chez Paree trotted out anything the guests ordered. But suddenly fatigue set in. The let-down was upon me. The emotional tension of a big fight plus the enormous physical strain of the third round when my arms were working like pistons had taken their toll. I was plain beat. A lot of sports writers wrote that I had to finish Durelle when I did, as I was obviously spent at the end of the fight. They remarked on my heavy breathing when I spoke into the microphone after the victory. Sure, I was spent, but according to my plan I could shoot the bolt in the third, and I did and I won. Finishing a tough man is not child's play, and even a fighter of twenty-two who throws sixteen or eighteen or twenty consecutive punches with full power behind them will feel exhausted. I guarantee if we had decided to go the full distance, I'd have made it. I've been around a little too long not to know what I'm doing in that ring. As for exhaustion coming on me because of my age, I say that's ridiculous. If I didn't think I was fit to fight, I'd quit. I never want to defraud the business that has finally made me wealthy.

# ROUND 13 EXCERPTS FROM MY DIARY

Every thread in the tapestry of life has a purpose, and I find there are a few loose strands in my story that don't fit snugly in the narrative and yet they should be woven in for what they are worth. Before I relate the further adventures of Archie Moore in Hollywood I would like to write down some of the odds and ends of living that have accumulated in my mental closet as I dug back through the years. . . .

When I was very young and had made my mind up to become a professional fighter, I also became an avid reader of anything and everything pertaining to boxing. In St. Louis, when I was keeping house for Knox James' mother, I had lots of free time, and in the mornings before the gym opened I would walk to the library and read about the great fighters of yesterday. As the years rolled on and I was pinching out a living in hundreds of towns, cities, and hamlets, I would seek out the library and if I saw a title on a book I hadn't read, I would steal it to read. The reason I stole them was that I would fight a bout and move on. I had such a love for my chosen profession that I felt I had to know all I could about it, and if the means to that end was filching a book here and there, I did it without a second thought. You must remember, too, that petty thievery was a commonplace thing to me in those days. Now, like a reformed drunk, I have a dread horror of stealing. Young men today who aspire to the prize ring have very little knowledge of the history of the game. They are groomed much too fast to get the TV buck, and they come and go with all the rapidity and distinction of subway trains. The legitimate theater used to have the "road," but they say that it is dead. So it is with exhibition tours. Fighters used to be able to win a tide and then cash in by touring thirty or so cities and fight the local pride and joy. No more. TV has finished that phase of the business, enriching the fighter beyond his wildest dreams, but it may be the ruination of the coming generation of boxers.

In the opening section of this book, I told of the events leading to my arrest and conviction as a juvenile delinquent. I was also arrested once in New York City on a violation of the Sullivan law, which is the illegal possession of concealed firearms. Here's how it happened and it should be put to music by Gilbert and Sullivan. After all, he wrote the law.

As you know, I am a jazz fanatic and my mania causes me to haunt record shops wherever I happen to be, and I frequent good jazz clubs on those occasions when I feel in the mood for some night life. I was living in Harlem, fighting for Mr. Jimmy Johnston, and I used to wander into a record store on 145$^{th}$ Street owned by a boy named Jimmy Knighton. He was a record collector and, although records were scarce during the war years, he'd dig up platters I hadn't heard. His shop was kind of run-down, but I thought that with his know-how the store could make a good go of it, if he only fixed it up. His answer was that he had visited his folks in Florida and lost most of his money gambling. But after we talked a while he asked me to buy half of the business. I still had the Chicken Shack and I wasn't exactly rich, but I did own a Buick convertible. Envisioning myself as a man with many financial interests, I sold the car and realized a little over $1,200. If my memory is correct, that was late in 1945. I gave Knighton the $1,200 and became his partner. I am a stickler for clean living and I began to mop the floor, paint the wall, and patch things up as best I could. I covered the shelves with material and tried to brighten up the display window. Meanwhile Jimmy hadn't paid any debts and was running deeper into the red.

One day a shipment came in, and among the albums was a new record that had just been released by Charley Brown and the Three Blazers. The bass player of the Three Blazers was Eddie Williams, who often stayed at my house in San Diego, so I knew him quite well. In those days album covers always had pictures of the musicians on them, and generally the bass player was placed in the middle. But on this album Eddie Williams was on the left, Charley Brown on the right and Johnny Moore in the center. While Jimmy and I were playing the album, we discussed the cover. Now Knighton thought himself a very hip cat, because he spent a lot of time in the old jazz joints along 52nd Street, but he incorrectly identified Eddie Williams as the man in the center. He got a little nasty when I corrected him and I suppose the guilt he suffered constantly about his gambling made him lose his temper. We argued, but I couldn't convince him. He offered to bet me I was wrong, and he started by naming $50 as the amount. I turned it down, explaining how well I knew Eddie Williams and thought it would be unfair to make such a bet. He insisted I was trying to back down, and now I began to egg him on. In the first place, I doubted if he had $50 and in the second place, I was now aware that Jimmy didn't care for me one bit. Now his rage was on the verge of violence, but some grain of sense kept his hands at his sides. I was amused more than anything, for I could tell the album cover had become secondary, and getting shut of me was his main aim. He raised the bet to a thousand dollars, and now I knew I had him. I'd win the bet and he'd be rid of me. I bet my half of the store against his. If I won, and I knew I would, I would keep the record collection and close the store. He agreed to this, but I still felt badly about it, and tried to jolly him by calling off the big bet and offering to bet a Coke on it. But now he was adamant. All the records, his half of the store.

Knowing him to be a sharp operator, I got a pencil and paper and wrote down the terms of the bet and who was betting on what, and had it notarized. It wasn't legal, of course, but it looked official to Jimmy, and the bet was on. He called several record companies in New York and each substantiated his statement. But the company that had pressed the album was in California, so I insisted that the people he had called were identifying Eddie Williams by his position on the album, just as he had. I got a couple of handsful of change and called California. I put Jimmy on the phone, and when he heard it was Eddie Williams on the left he almost fainted. He hung up the phone and went through to the back of the store where he lived. I began to stack my new records. Suddenly, I heard a loud *bang!* and didn't know what to do. I didn't think he'd shot himself. On the contrary, I actually thought he was going to shoot me, and the gun had gone off while he was loading it. But the acrid smell of smoke reached me now, and I went back and tried the door. The latch was on. I took a knife and opened it. Knighton was lying across the bed, and the window was wide open. I rushed back into the store and phoned for the police.

The police arrived and rushed in with their pistols drawn. They flipped Knighton over and there was absolutely nothing wrong with him. The smell of gun smoke was still hanging in the air. Now the cops began to look for the gun. They poked around, kicking things over and generally messing the place up. They kept asking me where the pistol was. I said I didn't know. I heard the shot, smelled the gun smoke, as they did, and assumed he threw it out the window.

Now the police asked me if I owned a gun, and I foolishly said I did. I had a locker with personal effects in the store, and in it was an old-fashioned stock-barreled gun I had had in California, absolutely legally. Without further thought, I opened the locker, and they arrested me. I was kept in jail a week and then sent to Riker's Island, where they gave me a bath and a uniform. I was about to get a number and a haircut when my fine was paid by a girlfriend of mine, Inez Jones. She had been scuffling around town trying to raise the money and had sold all her furniture to do so. I felt like the luckiest man in the world, as Riker's Island is not a tropical paradise.

Nothing more happened to me or to Knighton, and my friends, Tommy Bell and "Flash" Gordon, saw to it that I had a lawyer in court. I took the records—I still have them—and he continued to run the store. I run into him from time to time and we say hello, but it was a bizarre episode in my life, and one that I thought of the night I entered the Waldorf to get the Boxing Writer's Award. I had come a long way from reform school, the C.C.C. camp and Riker's Island. When you think about it, it's amazing. This is a great country, all right.

Shortly after my encounter with the law, my mother wired me $50, and "Flash" Gordon and I got on a train for California. We used literally every cent we had between us for our fares and we had absolutely no money left over to buy any food. Now it takes three days by train to California and soon after we changed trains in Chicago, our stomachs began to call for help. "Flash" and I were pretending we didn't hear when the then-Lightweight Champion, Bob Montgomery, his sparring partner, Dusty Brown, and his secretary, Norman Henry, came down the aisle from their drawing room in another car. They were on their way to the dining car, but they all stopped to chat with us.

Bob was going to fight some over-the-weight exhibitions in the West and he was trying to pick up a few extra pounds by eating Hershey chocolate bars. There he was standing right in front of our eyes and stomachs, going through a whole carton of chocolate bars. Of course, Bob had no idea of our situation, and we were too proud to let him know, so pretty soon he moved off to the diner, munching away on his chocolate bars. Norman Henry lagged behind for a minute, and I thought he was going to say something. But then he just sort of shook his head and went down the aisle after Bob.

"Flash" and I looked at each other and, feeling as bad as we did, we just had to laugh. I think we were almost hysterical. I know I was. Finally, I said to "Flash" that I would never forget this incident. Here I was, a top contender for years, and I didn't even have a nickel for a chocolate bar. I promised "Flash" that if I didn't lie right down in my seat and die before we got to California that someday I would be champion of the world.

Well, of course, I was able to make good that light headed promise, and shortly before my first fight with Yvon Durelle I ran into Bob Montgomery and Norman Henry again and told them the whole story. Norman told me that he had thought perhaps something was wrong, but he didn't want to ask because he had too much respect for me and was afraid I would think he was trying to be smart. I told him that he would never know how close I had come to begging him for one of Bob's chocolate bars. Yes, sir, I've been way down at the bottom in my life, and now I'm on the top; but I've never forgotten the days when things didn't go so well, and I've never forgotten all the good people who believed in me and helped me.

Incidentally, Norman Henry is one of the people who helps me out at the Salt Mine when I'm in training. Norman is a fine fellow, who manages fighters himself when he's not with me and manages fighters when he is with me. To those who believe in reincarnation and former lives on earth you can understand Norman when I say that at the dawn of civilization three men were very busy. One, as he watched lightning strike wood, saw the possibilities of fire. Another came rolling into the cave one day, having invented the wheel. And Norman? Well, Norman was asleep. He'd already invented the bed.

Since I have turned professional I have avoided fights outside the ring. People are always curious as to what would happen if a fighter got in a fight in a bar or on a street corner. I know what would happen. The man fighting with him would stand a good chance of being seriously hurt, and the fighter could break his hand, his main tool for earning his living. I have heard much talk that if a fighter does get into a fight the judge will throw the book at him, because his fists, being trained, are lethal weapons. I say I will never know about this, but I do know that I am allowed to defend myself if provoked, and that goes whether I'm a fighter or a doctor. I can usually avoid the tough drunk who screws up his courage to belt the champ to see if I can take it, or the pest who argues abusively, knowing I won't hit him. I walk away. But I do recall an evening in San Diego when a friend of mine and I were strolling casually down Broadway in San Diego. Five Marines, on the town, came towards us. They were singing and had their arms linked, forcing everyone to move around them. It didn't mean much to me, and I would have moved, as they were entitled to an evening's fun. But then the sudden, familiar sneer came through the air when I heard one Marine say loudly to his buddies, "Gettin' so you can't find room on the street on account of these spades."

Five to one are fairly good odds and out of the corner of my eye I saw my pal reaching for his pocket. I pushed him back out of the action, and raised my other palm up as though I was begging off. I balled my right into a fist and belted the second Marine from the left. He flew out of the formation, and my left hook caught the first Marine. The other three backed away and began talking and apologizing, but we didn't stay to listen. We beat it before the Shore Patrol arrived. Being a civilian and a Negro in a military town isn't the best of all possible worlds. But that was the only time I lost my temper, and it was a flare of rage that isn't apt to happen again. The more I learn about people the more easygoing I become.

I had another fight I'm ashamed of and that was against Len Morrow, the second time I fought him. In our first fight, I landed a low punch and extended both arms in apology. While I was wide open he threw a sneak right-hand shot that hit me square in the kisser. A year later, I fought him in Toledo and punched him into the hospital. In the seventh round I knew I had him and could put him away at any time. But I was mean and angry at him, so I waited until the tenth. But I was a little too mean. He got a concussion and nearly died. He has never been any good in the ring since then. I'm sorry for that.

On August 20, 1955, I married Joan Hardy. We now have two adorable daughters, 'Rene and baby Joan. She is my fifth wife. I have already written about the first, and the reason I have not gone into any detail about the other marriages is a simple one. I do not really think they are of interest, and I am now happily married, and some day my children will read this book, so I beg the gift of reticence on this point. I will say that I am sure some people may wonder whether

Catherine Turner came back into my life after my second break-up with Mattie. She did, but I married another girl before I got back with Catherine. She was a wonderful person.

Joan was a New York model and later worked in a tax attorney's office in downtown Manhattan. Her sister is Mrs. Sidney Poitier, wife of the famous and wonderful actor. I met Joan on a blind date. A mutual friend brought me to her apartment one evening. It was a lucky night for me. Through prize fighting I have met women, and because of prize fighting I have lost them. Women do not seem to resent husbands who work in banks, offices or any so-called "regular jobs," but athletes and people in show business are open to a lot of criticism from wives. The long separations when I am in training or boxing exhibitions in foreign lands cause wifely complaints, and not without reason. But boxing is my life, and I now have a wife who understands this. I never did have this understanding before. I went with Joan for a long time, and it was time I needed, for I had myself pegged a loser in the marriage department. But I finally asked Joan to marry me. I had never asked a girl to do that before. Either they had asked me, or it seemed like the thing to do at the time. I am a confirmed family man now, and the life I am living is solely a life for my wife and children, and I certainly like it that way.

All sports fans like to talk about the great men of their favorite sport, and people are always asking me who my favorite fighters are. I never saw Joe Gans, but from what I've read and heard I'd say my all-time great was the Old Master.

Joe Louis is the best heavyweight I've seen in action. John Henry Lewis was the best light heavyweight, but if anyone wants to dispute this and throw my name in, I'll listen to the discussion with rapt attention. The best middleweight was Sugar Ray Robinson, the best welterweight was Charlie Brady. Ike Williams is my pick for the best lightweight; bantamweight, Harold Dade; and flyweight, Earl Perez.

There are four more fighters I would like to mention. Two of them, Barney Ross and Fritzi Zivic, belong on anybody's list of greats. And at the top of my own list, the top, mind you, I put Henry

Armstrong. My last favorite is Sandy Saddler. I rate Sandy as one of the greatest punchers I ever saw, but if I had handled Sandy at the beginning I would have changed his style. I would have made him hard to hit by teaching him to use that fantastically long reach. They never would have hit him, and with his punch he would have become the greatest of them all. He did pretty well as it was. For a long time he was ahead of me on knockouts, and I believe he is still third in line. An automobile accident that caused injury to his eyes forced him to quit, so there is no telling how high that mark might have been.

Young fellows are always approaching me, asking advice on becoming a professional prize fighter. The way I look at it you've got to want to be a fighter 100 percent. Want it more than anything else in life. It's like this. In every five-year period there are about three thousand boys who want to be fighters. Only ten of these become champions. Think of it. Only ten in five years. Ten out of three thousand. One out of every three hundred. It's like having two hundred and ninety-nine strikes against you before you start. That's the way I look at it. Me, I always wanted to be a fighter more than anything else.

If you, as a young aspiring fighter, don't intend to go all out, then don't start. The penalty for losing is too much. It's terrible, because here's the thing—you can fight four or five years and you wind up a nonentity; you wind up with headaches you might carry to the grave; you wind up forfeiting much valuable time that could have been used establishing yourself in a trade or a profession. And in the years you are learning that trade or profession you are not getting hit. Contact sports are for determined people. You can fail playing baseball and go out and get another job but after being beaten around in boxing it is often tough to land a job, especially if you have the marks of your former work all over your face. So my advice to young fighters is this. . . . If you're so unsure you've got to ask me about fighting, stay away from it! It's just like what old J. P. Morgan said when someone asked him how much money you'd have to have to afford a yacht. "Young man, if you have to ask, you can't afford it."

# ROUND 14 A PRICE ON MY HEAD

Anyone with my measurements, 19, 12 and 48 (biceps, forearm and chest), ought to be a cinch for Hollywood. But the offers never came, streaks of gray began to appear, and I had about given up my hope of becoming a star of the silver screen. But one day, while I was training for the Durelle fight, I drove my wife and daughters from the Salt Mine to my home in San Diego. I had a cup of tea and was ready to leave for the return drive when I got the phone call that opened the door to what might possibly be a new career for me. A friend called to say an appointment had been made for me to see Sam Goldwyn, Jr., a producer, and a director named Michael Curtiz. It came so suddenly I simply said, "Oh," and hung up to tell my wife Joan what had happened.

"They want me to play the part of Jim, the slave, in a movie called *Huckleberry Finn.*"

"Archie," she said, "I read that book in school. It's by Mark Twain, but I wonder about you playing Jim. It's apt to bring a lot of criticism down on you. You know how all of us feel about handkerchief head parts."

Joan was referring to parts played in movies by Negroes who roll their eyes, faint passing graveyards and always have dice and a straight razor in their pockets. The "Yassuh, boss"-type role. I dislike that stereotype heartily. But *Huckleberry Finn* was a period picture.

Slavery was distasteful to Mark Twain, and Joan told me the slave Jim had dignity and integrity. A great deal of Jim's ignorance had been surmounted by native intelligence and resourcefulness. We agreed a fast trip to Los Angeles couldn't hurt and I made my plans to take a day off training just before we broke camp for Montreal.

Mr. Goldwyn and Mr. Curtiz explained the plot of the picture to me and both seemed enthusiastic about my possibilities. They knew I had to leave the following day to go East, but said they would send a script to Canada as soon as it was finished. I had a pleasant day at the studio and was given the usual tour and met whatever celebrities that were working that day. The fact that I hadn't run 6 miles that morning nor boxed was weighing on my conscience, but strong as that was, I practiced escapology from Mr. Conscience and had a fine lunch.

I mentioned the movie to the members of our party during the jet flight to New York and then forgot about it. About a week before the fight finally took place the script arrived and I read it. I read it over and over and memorized my lines, which amounted to about sixteen pages of the script. My main objection was the constant use of the word "nigger." It was a common word in those days, too common, but I felt it unnecessary to use it as often as they did. When Joan arrived in Montreal I had her read the script and she agreed with me. But she thought the script could be fixed easily enough to overcome my complaint. I now had another reason to beat poor Yvon, and after the fight I was prepared to return to the coast and try and land the part. We flew to New York on the first leg of the trip only to learn of the death of my niece, who was the daughter of Joan's older sister. In the face of my happiness, this tragedy was numbing. An automobile had struck her down on her way home from school. We stayed in New York until the funeral was over and Joan had had a chance to offer consolation to her sister. We flew directly to Los Angeles to attend a fight, and I made an appointment with Mr. Goldwyn.

Mike Curtiz was at the meeting, too, and when I mentioned that I didn't want to play an Uncle Tom role they both agreed with me. Just as Joan had said, they quickly pointed out that the script could easily be changed. In the final screenplay, the word is only used once and then not directly to me. I am chopping wood outside the house of the woman who owns me, and Huck's pap is trying to get $500 from her. When she refuses, saying she hasn't got $500, Huck's pap says, "You've got that nigger there. Sell him." This motivates my running away. I overhear the conversation, and being afraid of what fate might befall me, I decide to try and escape to a free state in the hope of making enough money to buy the freedom of my wife and child.

In another scene, when the steamboat picks me and Huck off the raft, the first mate says, "It's mighty strange—a Nigra." Since we cannot overlook the origins of a word, and the fact that it was commonplace during the time-setting of the movie, I agreed to these two lines. The only racial objection I got at the time was from Jet magazine. I think the people there will approve of the picture when they see it. I hope so. I like the magazine and it has many, many readers.

With the removal of the script difficulties, it now remained for Curtiz to decide whether or not I could act. I was sorry he had never "caught" me at the many weigh-ins I had performed at, because I had been reviewed by sports writers as a thespian of the first water on those occasions. A screen test was set up for the following day. I took the scene I was to do and went back to my hotel to study the lines for my debut.

This was a happy crossroads in my life. I had a chance to continue being Archie Moore with identification even after I left the ring. The small spark of identification that boxing had kindled way back in the C.C.C. camp was relit by this opportunity. I thought, too, of Canada Lee, who had been one of the finest actors, white or black, that I had ever seen. He, too, was an ex-pug. Canada was forced out of fighting by an eye injury. He was an exception, as most other fighters who were wooed by Hollywood played tough guy or prize-fighting roles. Here I had a chance to play a slave in a film based on an American classic. I felt more tension that night than I ever have felt before an important fight. I was at the studio two hours ahead of time, walking through the scene by myself. It was a scene on a raft where I talk to Huck about values as we float down the Mississippi.

Finally, the director was satisfied with the way the set looked and the lighting. "Places!" was called and I was on. I did the scene and it was like a fight. I heard the first word just as you feel the first punch and the next thing was the bell ending the round, the voice of Mike Curtiz saying, "That's it—cut!" The boy playing Huckleberry Finn in the scene was crying. The technicians and other members of the crew were crying and yelling and applauding. Curtiz and Goldwyn were beaming. I was in. I made it. I was later told that a reaction like this was rare indeed. It was one of the happiest days of my life. I called Joan and told her the good news.

I had seen people like Andy Devine, Buster Keaton and John Carradine many times on the screen, so the pleasure of working with these people was really terrific for me. Mickey Shaughnessy, Tony Randall and great little Eddie Hodges all helped me, and it was a ball.

Ingemar Johansson came to visit our set and we all posed for publicity pictures with him. He was playing a part in a war movie, and so the two actors posed for pictures side by side. It must have made the membership of the Screen Actor's Guild scream in horror. I greatly admire John Carradine. He is an actor's actor. When he is called, he gets up from his chair, saunters over, does his scene and then returns to read his paper, unconcerned with what is happening around him. He seldom had to do a scene more than once and he gave me a few tips that really made sense.

I must confess the applause I received for the test made me overconfident about this acting bit, and a few days later they had to make a scene five times with me to get it right. I stopped the nonsense right then and resumed the habit of getting to the lot much earlier than the call, to walk through my scenes, so I was letter-perfect for each day's work. It wasn't hard for me, since I'm so used to getting up earlier than most people, even actors. They carefully showed me how to hit my marks. These are chalk marks so situated that the actor must stay right there in order for the lights and camera focus to work perfectly. This was duck soup for me. Long ago I trained myself to know every inch of the canvas in a ring from any angle (even horizontal). At any time I know exactly how many steps it is to my corner or to a neutral corner. I know when the rope is directly behind me, so marks were understandable to me, and one hurdle was over before it caused trouble.

I lived in Beverly Hills at the Chateau Marmont, which is a favorite spot with actors. It is right on the Sunset Strip, and I drove from there to the studio every morning and drove home to San Diego weekends. I loved every minute of it even when Doc Kearns visited and told me to hurry up with this foolishness, as we still had some fighting to do. Hollywood was old stuff to Doc, for he and Jack Dempsey had made a serial there many years before, and Doc said it held a record as the worst picture ever made. I don't know whether he was hinting I might break Dempsey's record, but underneath it all Doc enjoyed the visit, because everyone had heard of him. He is a legend in his own time.

Friends of mine dropped in, and when the day's work was done the professional actors would crowd around the professional fight group. They were fascinated by our profession and we were fascinated by theirs. I refought many fights with added help from my trainers who were there, and when musician friends would stop by we'd have impromptu jazz during the lunch break and at the end of the day. It was all fun and it was a great experience working with a man like Curtiz. He is a perfectionist, and I like that. In my business it pays to be a perfectionist. There is no other way.

When a rough cut of the film was ready, Sam Goldwyn, Jr., had a sneak preview and invited my wife and me to see it. It was held in a regular neighborhood theater, and as we had arrived early, I sat through a so-called spectacle which, I was told, was cleaning up at the box office. I'm not a motion-picture critic, but I guarantee *Huckleberry Finn* is a hundred times better than this idiocy.

The reaction of the audience was fine, and there were smiles on the faces of all of us connected with the pro duction. In the lobby, fans soon recognized me and crowded around to say hello and get an autograph. They were using the cards placed in the lobby for their written comment about the movie. But Sam and Mike were pleased, anyway. This was the kind of enthusiasm they wanted. I had often left a fight arena to find a crowd outside, but this, somehow, was different. For the first time, I really felt like an actor. A lot of those people didn't even know I was a prize fighter. They just liked me up there on the screen. Boy, that was okay with me. I signed and beamed and probably would have stood there until the porter left the theater if I hadn't been dragged away. The excitement was so great that when we left the restaurant after the show I had to pull the car off the road and grab forty winks before continuing the drive home.

I am anxious for all my friends to see this picture so they can see for themselves that I wasn't put in the picture as a freak attraction to sell tickets. I honestly think I turned in a performance and not an appearance. I am anxious for my brother-in-law, Sidney Pokier, to see it, as I respect his great talent and would appreciate his criticism. It will come as no surprise to you that I hope my life is portrayed on the screen. I don't believe they will allow me to play myself, because I doubt if I can make the weight that Archie Moore of the C.C.C. camp carried. But I can be a technical adviser on the prize fighting aspects of the story and get to spend some more happy days on a movie lot, where work, to me, is like play.

# ROUND 15 EXIT LAUGHING

As I am writing now, it is March 22, 1960, and I'm waiting to sign a contract to defend my title against Erich Schoeppner, the German champion. If I win, I've been promised a match against the winner of the Johansson-Patterson heavyweight title fight. And after that?

A man hates to predict what he will do in the future. So much can happen. The unexpected, the unwanted or the surprise bonus. But at least I know I have a future. That, in itself, tells me I've made it. The boy who used to hack weeds in the Missouri sun and dream of money and glory achieved both. Prize fighting enabled me to see the world, meet wonderful people and give security to my family. Being a fighter and a champion has meant everything to me. It's meant that I can go into restaurants or to banquets and be recognized as Archie Moore. Sure, recognized by people who wouldn't even look at me if I wasn't champ, but that's part of the identification, too. I'm not easily fooled by them anymore. And the money . . . it's awfully nice if you can go all the way; if you get to the end of that long road, maybe you're gonna find that pot of gold. It makes all the difference. I don't care what you say, this is a civilization based on money, isn't that right? To be recognized you've got to succeed economically. And another thing, it isn't *just* the fame, the recognition and the money. It's a sense of achievement, too. The knowledge that you can go in there and be a winner. The inner feeling that you're good at your business. My business is fighting. I've had 206 fights, won 176 of them, drew six and won 128 by knockouts. I'm a proud man. I hold my head high.

But if pride goeth before a fall I've got a lot of things going for me to soften the blow. About the time this book comes out, *Huckleberry Finn* should be playing in the theaters. That means Archie Moore, the actor, can take over if the opportunity arises. Or maybe one of the boys I teach will hit on all cylinders and Archie Moore, boxing manager and publicist, can take over. Or as the years go by and the improvements mount at the Salt Mine, the job of providing security will fall on the shoulders of Archie Moore, health ranch proprietor. And all of this has come from boxing.

Some people can trace the beginnings of their ambition to little things, but I know mine came from a big thing. The love of my late uncle and my auntie, Willie Pearl Moore. It was so big I just couldn't step around it. It forged my determination to make good, to be some body. It seems to me there is a startling lack of affection in this world, and it seems to be chic to lie on a couch and blame your failures on your mother or father. Get with it, you are what you make yourself, barring accident or ill health.

The other day out at the Salt Mine I had a humorous thought. I could make the place into a green pasture for old fight managers. It wouldn't be too hard. I know what they require to make them happy. Plenty of cigars, free food and lots of hot coffee. An ample supply of fighters to cheat and rob to amuse themselves. Here and there a shady character from the underworld to make deals with. I'd have to build a few more rings, because I'd like to watch their beady little eyes light up as the sparring partners bounce off the canvas. Each manager will have a docile tiger he can call stupid, and he'll be permitted to take the fighter's lunch and eat it himself. Oh, it'll be a paradise, all right. But it's just a whimsical thought, because even if I did it, they'd be so suspicious none of them would check in.

I look back over the years and think of the tough ones I fought; Shorty Hogue, Ron Richards, Eddie Booker, Rocky Marciano and many others. But I think, too, with some regret, that I never fought Sugar Ray Robinson. Both of us are punching boxers, and it would still be a great match. Each of us has aged some, so that part is even. Besides being a glorious payday, it would settle once and for all who is the better man. I say I can whip Ray, and I'm sure he says the same thing about me.

Recently, after the mess and scandal of the first Johansson-Patterson fight promotion, I was contacted by Steve Masters, the discount house king, who had conceived a gigantic plan. He had formed a small syndicate of very respectable businessmen to promote two fights.

His feeling was that with an open and honest promotion boxing would be both better and more attractive and Steve's idea was to have Patterson and Johansson fight on the same card with Moore versus Robinson. Instead of televising this in theaters, he would televise it in arenas all across the country at very nominal prices, no reserved seats outside the Yankee Stadium in New York. The total take for a boxing card like this might well have hit twenty million dollars. For that day is coming. With worldwide television not too far away, the million-dollar gate that gave Doc Kearns his aura of wizardry will literally be a drop in the bucket. Knowing that I am sentimental about money, you can readily understand why I'd like to be champ for another ten years. The last part of Steve's plan was to certify a bank in each town to sell the arena tickets. This would have assured the fighters an honest count. That part of his idea was a real dream. It ain't ever gonna happen.

Jimmy Johnston was good to me and Doc Kearns always gets me the best possible deal. All the other managers I've had were just flesh peddlers. But that's nothing new. They've acted that way since the days of old Rome when the managers patted the backs of the gladiators and shoved them out to the lions.

I think of the myriad towns I have been in. Of lying on my back in a steamy, cheap hotel room, listening to the engine switching box cars back and forth beneath my window. I'm glad of the thought. I can enjoy my luxurious bed tonight all the more. I think of rotten, starchy meals designed to fill my belly at minimum cost, and I shake my head and smile as I cut my sirloin. I remember sitting on the hard bed of a truck for mile after mile, and I relax as I ease behind the wheel of my convertible. I recall standing in the hall of the reform school at stiff attention as a man chastises a child with a 4-inch leather strap, and I pick up my beautiful daughters and kiss them lest they forget that love and life go hand in hand.

There's a feeling of finality when you write a book about yourself, but I hope to live another fifteen chapters. Maybe not as exciting as these have been to me, but excitement is a wine for the young, bubbling with prom ise. At my age, I like a little still wine that has body and taste and security.

My wife has never said so, but I know she is looking forward to the day I hang up my gloves and climb down out of the ring. I know it sounds cozy. I have all my trophies shined and in a case. My pictures on the wall, my scrapbooks and my many friends, but I have one other thing, and that's what bothers me. I'm still very much alive. I'm still the old mongoose in there trying to outwit and out hit the younger guys. I'm like the drunk in the bar who just wants one more for the road. I want one more knockout to add to my record and then just one more after that. Some people say it's great when a man retires undefeated champion. But the word champion means I must be beaten. A champion should fight to the finish and go out with his hands cocked just as he came in. It's the proper exit and I think it may be mine.

When I retire I want to get very, very fat just once. Not for the sake of being fat but to put away a mountain of mashed potatoes, a barnyard full of fried chicken, gallons of lemonade and sherbet, Herbert. But then, of course, I'll go back on my diet and stay in shape, because fat is a killer of men.

I'm gonna stay up late and inhale the fumes of good jazz in nice, smoky night clubs with good jazz combos. I'm gonna sleep late in the mornings and never run again. I'll burn all my training clothes and hang my gloves way up high out of reach.

Later on I'll bore my little girls with stories of fighting when they'd rather be talking about the school dance. But it will be fun when they realize a lot of boys will want to meet them to shake hands with Archie Moore, the fighter their fathers saw way back when. Then one day my wife will hide my dusty scrapbooks and my picture albums and I'll have to walk down to the gym every day and shoot the bull with the other old-timers, as I watch the kids and think to myself that I could've beaten all of them in my time. That's an old fighter's privilege. I've met many who believe they could have beaten me and I always agree with them. No purse on the line, you see.

Joan and I want to travel. I'd like to take my children to all the places all over the globe where I've had fights. I'd like to visit countries I haven't seen. South Africa, for instance. I've been corresponding with people who live there, and as a Negro I'd like to see for myself what is happening. It might not be pleasant but I would like to know. I'd also like to be around the day the strife gets settled and kids can go to school again. I once heard a line that somebody told me a writer named Art Franklin said. The gist of it was, "The white men say all men are created equal and then they hate the black man for believing it." It has a hard, cold ring to it, but perhaps in my time it will change for the better.

I'm going to take an active part in whatever youth programs are sponsored in my community. I believe in boxing as a sport for sport's sake, and I want to help organizing boxing teams and teaching youngsters the only art of boxing—self-defense. A man who can defend himself has two legs to stand on and in this world you've got to hang in there; you've got to stand up for yourself, for what you think is right.

I have been bilked, cheated and hoodwinked but when I picked up my lucky penny it was heads up and smiling. My home is a showplace in San Diego and I planned it that way. The security of a home to a rover like me cannot be understood by most people. I have a reverence for the land that goes back to my Mississippi roots, and an obsession about owning my own roof that stems from my early days when Uncle Cleveland was forced by circumstance to move from place to place.

I want my little girls to have things my dear sister never could have. I want to have room at the table and a bed upstairs for my kinfolk and my close friends. I want music and laughter in my home. I want what every man wants—contentment and peace of mind.

I still say I'm forty-three years old and I hope I run my Biblical string out. I won't promise that I'll still be fighting then, but if God stays in my corner, they'll be able to print on my tombstone, "Here lies Archie Moore—smiling."

## WEIGH-OUT: MY SECRET DIET

The basic idea for reducing that I discovered for myself in Australia has been refined through constant experimenting, and I can now guarantee its effectiveness for anyone in good health who sincerely wishes to lose weight.

The object is to shrink the stomach. This cuts down your appetite and insures maintenance of your new, lighter weight. A parallel objective is to maintain your strength, which too many diets tend to sap.

Almost all of us who are weight-conscious are now aware of cholesterol. The body manufactures fat which clings to the linings of the blood veins and is a dangerous threat to the heart. I have found a way of keeping this danger down to a minimum. I drink 4 ounces of sauerkraut juice with a teaspoon of lemon juice mixed in. I heat this to make it more palatable. It is a drink, I am afraid, that you must accustom yourself to, but if taken faithfully it becomes a daily routine and not a chore.

Naturally, I advocate chewing my meat and not swallowing the bulk. But you might say I am a professional weight loser, and the average person does not have to practice this to lose whatever pounds are set as his goal.

My theory of relaxism goes hand in hand with the diet. No dieting is pleasant, but when the weight is gone the reward can be seen. Relax about your diet. Don't talk about it, because you are naturally talking about food or the lack of food. During the working day, quite naturally, your mind is occupied and the diet will seem easy enough. In your free time, try to keep your mind equally active. Most of us have an escape hatch to allow us to relax. Perhaps you would like to catch up on reading or write letters you've put off answering. Movies, TV and music all help to keep your mind away from food.

When you embark on a diet it is well to warn people close to you, for dieting may make you irritable. This varies with the intensity of your diet, and if you are engaged in a courtship, stay fat until the honeymoon is over. I diet at a training camp, and it is a fact known to all sports fans that fighters in training live alone and sleep alone. I'm sure that my wife Joan wouldn't put up with the grouch that I change into during my training. The men who work for me tolerate my nasty ways, but they understand what is causing it and somehow work around me. It becomes doubly difficult when sports writers visit me, for I must curb my tongue. During my training period at North Adams for the Marciano fight, I almost got the reputation of being a smart aleck with a big head. A bad disposition can do this for you.

The kraut juice will also help you keep regular bowel habits. I am sincerely against pill-taking of any kind. I do supplement my diet with vitamin tablets, but vitamins are needed by all of us, for none of us can get as much sun as my friends the aborigines. The elimination of bodily waste is essential to good health. The feeling of sluggishness will disappear and your mental processes will be stimulated as soon as your elimination is regulated.

As a nondrinker I think alcohol is bad, diet or no diet. But for those of you who drink and wish to diet too, I say you must consider the calorie count of whatever you imbibe and make some food sacrifice to balance this. You will only be fooling yourself if you don't. The first pounds off are bloat. And bloat results from liquid intake. By cutting your liquids down as far as you can, you will speed up your reduction. In training I drink a pint of water a day, which is kept in the refrigerator, so I can gauge what is left. I carry a canteen of water with me when I run but I only use it to wash my mouth, as I run on dusty mountain roads and have to breathe heavily, which causes a terrible dryness.

If I were to drink a cold can of beer during my training, it would mean running 4 miles to get rid of it. This keeps me away from beer. I love watermelon but that, too, means hard tough work, so I stay away from Georgia ham.

Sleep is important to a person dieting. The body is under pressure when you're reducing and sleep helps you fight the strain. Sleep, too, fights your irritability. Lack of sleep will precipitate a grouchy outlook.

Before undertaking a strenuous diet be sure and have a checkup by your doctor. For many people dieting can be dangerous. And, during your checkup, have your doctor determine what your proper weight should be. Charts that say a man so tall should weigh so much are not accurate, because they generalize. Each person's frame is different. I am short by average standards and yet I carry a lot of weight. But my muscles are above normal and I need more weight than another man exactly tall as me.

If your heart belongs to Daddy, let him worry about it, but if your heart is your own, make sure it is in good shape before dieting. My diet is not injurious and will take off weight, but I want to emphasize the necessity for being in good health before trying to lose weight by any method or any diet. See your doctor first.

Stay away from coffee breaks and any between-meal snacks. Here again you are only kidding yourself. Coffee is liquid and also a nerve-irritant. You don't need more than your just share while dieting. Candies and sweets are naturally taboo.

You must be positive you want to lose weight or you'll find yourself cheating in little ways. Once you are positive you'll find it easier to stick until your goal is achieved. Don't weigh yourself every day, but do weigh yourself once a week. Daily progress may be discouraging, but by noting your weight weekly you'll see an encouraging difference.

If, after coming to the end of my diet, you want to lose more weight, repeat the last week of the diet. Think thin and go to it! Everybody loves a fat man but a fat man. Good luck.

# MY FOUR-WEEK DIET

Begin each day with the kraut drink: 1 cup of hot kraut juice with 1 tablespoon lemon juice added.

You may add one teaspoon of sugar to your coffee or tea if you must have it. No cream.

I drink my egg raw in orange juice, but the menus contain alternate suggestions for people who cannot take this.

Throughout the diet, the vitamin water (left from the cooked vegetables) is taken as part of the diet. Do not drink or snack between meals.

Erect posture is important to digestion. Sit upright while eating.

Chew each piece thoroughly when eating meats such as steaks or chops; discard as much of the bulk as you can.

## FIRST WEEK

### MONDAY

*Breakfast:* 1 cup kraut drink
1 poached egg
1 thin slice whole wheat bread
1 tablespoon honey
3 strips crisp bacon
1 cup black coffee or tea
8-ounce glass water

*Lunch:* 1 slice whole wheat bread, plain or toasted
Apple or orange
8-ounce glass buttermilk
8-ounce glass water
1 cup black coffee or tea

*Dinner:* 1 cup vegetable soup

large T-bone steak, rare to medium-rare (follow chewing instructions; the elimination of the useless bulk hastens the shrinking of your stomach, thereby lessening its demands for food)
half head of lettuce
6 raw carrot sticks
1 cup of spinach and broth
fresh fruit cup (avoid canned fruit because of the sweetened syrup)
8-ounce glass water
1 cup of coffee or tea

TUESDAY

*Breakfast:* 1 cup kraut drink
1 slice whole wheat bread or toast
1 tablespoon honey
1 boiled egg
broiled lamb kidney
1 cup of coffee or tea
8-ounce glass water

*Lunch:* one-fourth cup raisins
1 slice whole wheat bread or toast
8-ounce glass buttermilk
1 cup of coffee or tea
8-ounce glass of water

*Dinner:* 1 cup clam chowder
2 lamb chops
2 boiled beets and tops (eat greens and broth) half head of lettuce
sliced apple
1 slice whole wheat bread
1 cup jello
8-ounce glass water
one cup of coffee or tea

**WEDNESDAY**

*Breakfast:* 1 cup kraut juice
1 slice whole wheat bread or toast
1 tablespoon honey
2 poached eggs
1 sliced orange
8-ounce glass of water
1 cup of coffee or tea

*Lunch:* 1 slice whole wheat bread or toast
8-ounce glass of buttermilk
1 cup of coffee or tea
8-ounce glass water

*Dinner:* 1 cup tomato soup
steak
one-half cup boiled parsnips
one-half cup peas
one-half head lettuce
5 radishes
half cup tapioca
1 cup coffee or tea
8-ounce glass of water

**THURSDAY**

*Breakfast:* 1 cup kraut drink
1 slice whole wheat bread
tablespoon of honey
2-egg omelet
1 cup of black coffee or tea
8-ounce glass of water

*Lunch:* 1 slice whole wheat bread or toast
8-ounce glass of buttermilk
1 cup of coffee or tea

8-ounce glass of water

*Dinner:* Small steak
1 cup broccoli and broth
1 cup coleslaw
1 slice whole wheat bread
one-half cup applesauce
1 cup of coffee or tea
8-ounce glass of water

**FRIDAY**

*Breakfast:* 1 cup of kraut drink
*1 small lamb chop (to be eaten, juices and bulk)
1 boiled egg
1 slice whole wheat bread or toast
1 tablespoon honey
1 cup black coffee or tea
8-ounce glass of water

*Lunch:* 1 slice of whole wheat bread or toast
8-ounce glass of buttermilk
1 cup of coffee or tea
8-ounce glass of water

*Dinner:* Average serving broiled fish
one-half cup of green beans
endive salad
1 piece whole wheat bread or toast
1 sliced orange
1 cup of coffee or tea
8-ounce glass of water

**SATURDAY**

*Breakfast:* 1 cup of kraut drink

---

* Poached egg may be substituted for meat course on Friday breakfast menu.

3 slices crisp bacon
1 poached egg
1 slice whole wheat bread or toast
1 tablespoon of honey
1 apple
1 cup of black coffee or tea
8-ounce glass of water

*Lunch:* 1 slice of whole wheat bread or toast
8-ounce glass of buttermilk
1 cup of coffee or tea
8-ounce glass of water

*Dinner:* 1 cup of spinach soup
2 broiled lamb chops
ten pods of okra
1 cup of turnip greens and broth
1 slice of whole wheat bread or toast
1 pear or other fruit in season
8-ounce glass of water

**SUNDAY**
*Breakfast:* 1 cup of kraut drink
broiled lamb kidney (bulk to be eaten)1 poached egg
1 slice of whole wheat bread or toast
1 tablespoon of honey
1 cup of black coffee or tea
8-ounce glass of water

*Lunch:* 1 slice of whole wheat bread or toast
8-ounce glass of buttermilk
1 cup of black coffee or tea
8-ounce glass of water

*Dinner:* 1 cup of chicken bouillon
1 slice calves' liver (bulk to be eaten)

one-half cup of succotash
one-half head of lettuce
6 raw carrot sticks
1 banana
1 cup of black coffee or tea
8-ounce glass of water

## SECOND WEEK

### MONDAY

*Breakfast:* 1 cup of kraut drink
3 strips of crisp bacon
1 egg omelet
6 prunes
1 slice of whole wheat bread or toast
1 tablespoon of honey
1 cup of black coffee or tea
8-ounce glass of water

*Lunch:* 1 slice of whole wheat bread
8-ounce glass of buttermilk
1 cup of black coffee or tea
8-ounce glass of water

*Dinner:* Average serving broiled fish
6 stalks asparagus and broth
1 slice of whole wheat bread or toast
one-half head of lettuce
one-fourth cup of raisins
1 cup of black coffee or tea
8-ounce glass of water

### TUESDAY

*Breakfast:* 1 cup of kraut drink
3 strips of bacon
1 boiled egg
1 slice of whole wheat bread or toast

1 tablespoon of honey
1 cup of black coffee or tea
8-ounce glass of water

*Lunch:* 1 slice of whole wheat bread or toast
8-ounce glass of buttermilk
1 cup of black coffee or tea
8-ounce glass of water

*Dinner:* Average serving of steak
1 cup of kale and broth
one-half head of lettuce
6 raw carrot sticks
two-thirds cup of custard
1 cup of black coffee or tea
8-ounce glass of water

**WEDNESDAY**

*Breakfast:* 1 cup of kraut drink
1 tablespoon of honey; 8-ounce glass buttermilk
1 cup of black coffee or tea
8-ounce glass of water

*Lunch:* 8-ounce glass of buttermilk
1 cup of black coffee or tea
8-ounce glass of water

*Dinner:* 8-ounce glass of buttermilk
1 cup of black coffee or tea
8-ounce glass of water

**THURSDAY**

*Breakfast:* 1 cup of kraut drink
2 strips of crisp bacon
1 poached egg

1 slice of whole wheat bread or toast
1 tablespoon of honey
1 apple
1 cup of black coffee or tea
8-ounce glass of water

*Lunch:* 1 slice of whole wheat bread or toast
8-ounce glass of buttermilk
1 cup of black coffee or tea
8-ounce glass of water

*Dinner:* 2 lamb chops
one-half cup of green beans and broth
one-half head of lettuce
4 carrot sticks
1 sliced orange
1 cup of black coffee or tea
8-ounce glass of water

**FRIDAY**
*Breakfast:* 1 cup of kraut drink
1 lamb chop (bulk to be eaten)
1 poached egg
3 kadota figs
1 slice of whole wheat bread or toast
1 tablespoon of honey
1 cup of black coffee or tea
8-ounce glass of water

*Lunch:* 8-ounce glass of buttermilk
1 cup of coffee or tea
8-ounce glass of water

*Dinner:* 1 cup of bouillon, tomato or beef
average serving broiled fish
2 boiled beets and broth

beet greens
one-fourth cup of raisins
1 cup of black coffee or tea
8-ounce glass of water

**SATURDAY**

*Breakfast:* 1 cup of kraut drink
2 strips crisp bacon
one-fourth cup scrambled eggs
1 slice whole wheat bread or toast, tablespoon of honey
1 cup of black coffee or tea
8-ounce glass of water

*Lunch:* 8-ounce glass of buttermilk
1 slice of whole wheat bread
1 cup of black coffee or tea
8-ounce glass of water

*Dinner:* average serving steak
2 slices broiled eggplant
one-half cup of green peas
one-half head of lettuce
raw fruit in season
1 cup of black coffee or tea
8-ounce glass of water

**SUNDAY**

*Breakfast:* 1 cup of kraut drink
2 crisp strips of bacon
1 poached egg
1 slice of whole wheat bread
1 tablespoon of honey
1 apple
1 cup of black coffee or tea

8-ounce glass of water

*Lunch:* 1 slice of whole wheat bread or toast 8-ounce glass of buttermilk
1 cup of black coffee or tea
8-ounce glass of water

*Dinner:* one-fourth pound calves' liver
one-half cup squash (boiled, drink broth) one-half head lettuce
one-half cup of jello
1 cup of coffee or tea
8-ounce glass of water

## THIRD WEEK

### MONDAY

*Breakfast:* 1 cup of kraut drink
1 small lamb chop (bulk to be eaten)
1 cup of scrambled eggs
3 kadota figs
1 slice whole wheat bread or toast
1 tablespoon of honey
1 cup of black coffee or tea
8-ounce glass of water

*Lunch:* 8-ounce glass of buttermilk
1 slice of whole wheat bread or toast
1 cup of black coffee or tea
8-ounce glass of water

*Dinner:* 1 cup of beef bouillon
average serving steak
1 cup mustard greens, or other available, and broth
one-half head of lettuce
2 tablespoons cottage cheese

one-half cup of fruit in season
1 cup of black coffee or tea
8-ounce glass of water

**TUESDAY**

*Breakfast:* 1 cup of kraut drink
1 poached egg
1 slice whole wheat bread or toast
1 tablespoon of honey
1 apple
1 cup of black coffee or tea
8-ounce glass of water

*Lunch:* 1 slice whole wheat bread or toast
8-ounce glass of buttermilk
1 cup of black coffee or tea
8-ounce glass of water

*Dinner:* three-fourth cup clam chowder
average serving salmon steak
three-fourth cup spinach and broth
1 globe artichoke
1 cup of jello
1 cup of black coffee or tea
8-ounce glass of water

**WEDNESDAY**

*Breakfast:* 1 cup of kraut drink
1 tablespoon of honey
8-ounce glass of buttermilk
1 cup of black coffee or tea
8-ounce glass of water

*Lunch:* 1 slice of whole wheat bread or toast
8-ounce glass of buttermilk
1 cup of black coffee or tea

8-ounce glass of water

*Dinner:* 1 slice of whole wheat bread or toast
8-ounce glass of buttermilk
1 apple
1 cup of black coffee or tea
8-ounce glass of water

**THURSDAY**

*Breakfast:* 1 cup of kraut drink
1 small lamb chop (bulk to be eaten)
2 poached eggs
1 slice whole wheat bread or toast
1 tablespoon of honey
1 banana
1 cup of black coffee or tea
8-ounce glass of water

*Lunch:* 1 slice whole wheat bread or toast
8-ounce glass of buttermilk
1 cup of black coffee or tea
8-ounce glass of water

*Dinner:* two-thirds cup of pea soup
average serving roast chicken
seven-eighths cup of broccoli and broth
1 cup of coleslaw
two-thirds cup of custard
1 cup of black coffee or tea
8-ounce glass of water

**FRIDAY**

*Breakfast:* 1 cup of kraut drink
1 slice of calves' liver (bulk to be eaten)

1 boiled egg
1 slice of whole wheat bread or toast
1 tablespoon of honey
1 apple
1 cup of black coffee or tea
8-ounce glass of water

*Lunch:* 1 slice of whole wheat bread or toast
8-ounce glass of buttermilk
1 cup of black coffee or tea
8-ounce glass of water

*Dinner:* average serving broiled fish
one-half cup of celery soup
one-half cup of parsnips and broth
one globe artichoke
2 tablespoons of cottage cheese
1 cup of raw fruit
1 cup of black coffee or tea
8-ounce glass of water

**SATURDAY**

*Breakfast:* 1 cup of kraut drink
1 slice of whole wheat bread or toast
1 tablespoon of honey
8-ounce glass of buttermilk
1 cup of black coffee or tea
8-ounce glass of water

*Lunch:* 1 slice of whole wheat bread or toast
8-ounce glass of buttermilk
1 cup of black coffee or tea
8-ounce glass of water

*Dinner:* 1 slice of whole wheat bread or toast
8-ounce glass of buttermilk

1 banana
1 cup of black coffee or tea
8-ounce glass of water

**SUNDAY**

*Breakfast:* 1 cup of kraut drink
one-half cup of cheese souffle
6 prunes
1 slice of whole wheat bread or toast
1 tablespoon of honey
1 cup of black coffee or tea
8-ounce glass of water

*Lunch:* 1 slice of whole wheat bread or toast
8-ounce glass of buttermilk
1 cup of black coffee or tea
8-ounce glass of water

*Dinner:* average portion roast beef
ten stalks asparagus
one-half head of lettuce
4 to six stalks of celery
2 tablespoons of cottage cheese
one-half cup of raw fruit
1 cup of black coffee or tea
8-ounce glass of water

## FOURTH WEEK

**MONDAY**

*Breakfast:* 1 cup of kraut drink
2 crisp slices of bacon
1 boiled egg
1 kadota fig
1 slice of whole wheat bread or toast
1 tablespoon of honey
1 cup of black coffee or tea

8-ounce glass of water

*Lunch:* 1 slice of whole wheat bread or toast
8-ounce glass of buttermilk
1 cup of black coffee or tea
8-ounce glass of water

*Dinner:* 1 cup of beef bouillon
6 to 1 2 large oysters or average serving broiled
fish one-half cup of mustard greens and broth one-half
head of lettuce
1 cup of jello
1 cup of black coffee or tea
8-ounce glass of water

**TUESDAY**

*Breakfast:* 1 cup of kraut drink
1 slice of whole wheat bread or toast
1 tablespoon of honey
8-ounce glass of buttermilk
1 cup of coffee or tea
8-ounce glass of water

*Lunch:* 1 slice of whole wheat bread or toast
8-ounce glass of buttermilk
1 cup of black coffee or tea
8-ounce glass of water

*Dinner:* 1 slice of whole wheat bread or toast
8-ounce glass of buttermilk
1 cup of black coffee or tea
8-ounce glass of water

**WEDNESDAY**

*Breakfast:* 1 cup of kraut drink
1 small lamb chop (bulk to be eaten)

1 poached egg
1 slice of whole wheat bread or toast
1 tablespoon of honey
1 banana
1 cup of black coffee or tea
8-ounce glass of water

*Lunch:* 1 slice of whole wheat bread or toast
8-ounce glass of buttermilk
1 cup of black coffee or tea
8-ounce glass of water

*Dinner:* 1 cup of vegetable soup
average serving roast chicken
two-thirds cup brussels sprouts and broth
one-half head of lettuce
one-fourth cup of raisins
1 cup of jello
1 cup of black coffee or tea
8-ounce glass of water

**THURSDAY**

*Breakfast:* 1 cup of kraut drink
1 slice of whole wheat bread or toast
8-ounce glass of buttermilk
1 tablespoon of honey
1 cup of black coffee or tea
8-ounce glass of water

*Lunch:* 1 slice of whole wheat bread or toast
8-ounce glass of buttermilk
1 cup of black coffee or tea
8-ounce glass of water

*Dinner:* 1 slice of whole wheat bread or toast
8-ounce glass of buttermilk

1 cup of black coffee or tea
8-ounce glass of water

**FRIDAY**

*Breakfast:* 1 cup of kraut drink
1 slice of calves' liver
6 prunes
1 slice of whole wheat bread or toast
1 tablespoon of honey
1 cup of black coffee or tea
8-ounce glass of water

*Lunch:* 1 slice of whole wheat bread or toast
8-ounce glass of buttermilk
1 cup of black coffee or tea
8-ounce glass of water

*Dinner:* average serving broiled fish
1 cup of tomato soup
one-half cup cauliflower and broth
6 pieces of endive
two tablespoons of cottage cheese
one-half cup of raw fruit
1 cup of black coffee or tea
8-ounce glass of water

**SATURDAY**

*Breakfast:* 1 cup of kraut drink
1 slice of whole wheat bread or toast
1 tablespoon of honey
8-ounce glass of buttermilk
1 cup of black coffee or tea
8-ounce glass of water

*Lunch:* 1 slice of whole wheat bread or toast
8-ounce glass of buttermilk

1 cup of black coffee or tea
8-ounce glass of water

*Dinner:* 1 slice of whole wheat bread or toast
8-ounce glass of buttermilk
1 apple
8-ounce glass of water

**SUNDAY**

*Breakfast:* 1 cup of kraut drink
broiled lamb kidney
1 boiled egg
1 slice of whole wheat bread or toast 1 tablespoon of honey
1 cup of black coffee or tea
8-ounce glass of water

*Lunch:* 1 slice of whole wheat bread or toast
8-ounce glass of buttermilk
1 cup of black coffee or tea
8-ounce glass of water

*Dinner:* 1 cup of beef bouillon
average portion of steak
one-half cup of turnip greens and broth
one-half cup of coleslaw
2 tablespoons cottage cheese
one-half cup of jello
1 apple
1 cup of black coffee or tea
8-ounce glass of water

After completing this diet, if you've been faithful to it, you will have lost from 10 to 12 pounds. If you must lose more weight, continue the diet for another month.

# FIGHT RECORD

| Date | Opponent | Result | Type | Round |
|---|---|---|---|---|
| September 3, 1935 | Billy Simms | Win | KO | 2 (4) |
| January 1, 1936 | Kid Pocahuntas | Win | KO | 3 (8) |
| July 14, 1936 | Murray Allen | Win | PTS | 6 |
| August 4, 1936 | Sammy Christian | Draw | PTS | 6 |
| September 30, 1936 | Murray Allen | Win | KO | 2 (6) |
| October 9, 1936 | Sammy Jackson | Win | PTS | 5 |
| January 5, 1937 | Mack Payne | Win | KO | 1 (8) |
| January 18, 1937 | Johnny Davis | Win | KO | 4 (8) |
| January 29, 1937 | Sammy Jackson | Draw | PTS | 8 |
| February 2, 1937 | Joe Huff | Win | KO | 3 (5) |
| March 23, 1937 | Ham Pounder | Win | KO | 2 (8) |
| April 9, 1937 | Charley Dawson | Win | PTS | 8 |
| April 23, 1937 | Carl Martin | Win | RTD | 1 (8) |
| May 28, 1937 | Doty Turner | Win | KO | 1 (8) |
| June 1, 1937 | Al Dublinsky | Win | KO | 3 (?) |
| July 21, 1937 | Frank Hatfield | Win | KO | 1 (8) |
| August 19, 1937 | Deacon Logan | Win | KO | 3 (5) |
| September 1, 1937 | Billy Adams | Loss | PTS | 8 |
| September 9, 1937 | Sammy Slaughter | Win | PTS | 10 |
| September 17, 1937 | Charley Dawson | Win | TKO | 5 (5) |
| November 9, 1937 | Chuck Vickers | Win | KO | 2 (10) |
| November 16, 1937 | Sammy Christian | Win | PTS | 5 |
| December 1, 1937 | Sammy Jackson | Win | KO | 8 (10) |
| January 7, 1938 | Karl Lautenschlager | Win | TKO | 2 (5) |
| May 20, 1938 | Jimmy Brent | Win | KO | 1 (6) |
| May 27, 1938 | Ray Vargas | Win | KO | 3 (10) |
| June 24, 1938 | Johnny Romero | Loss | PTS | 10 |
| July 22, 1938 | Johnny Sikes | Win | KO | 1 (10) |
| August 5, 1938 | Lorenzo Pedro | Win | PTS | 10 |
| September 2, 1938 | Johnny Romero | Win | KO | 8 (10) |
| September 16, 1938 | Frank Rowsey | Win | TKO | 3 (10) |
| September 27, 1938 | Tom Henry | Win | TKO | 4 (6) |
| October 19, 1938 | Bobby Yannes | Win | TKO | 2 (10) |
| November 22, 1938 | Ray Lyle | Win | KO | 2 (10) |
| December 7, 1938 | Bob Turner | Win | KO | 2 (8) |
| January 20, 1939 | Jack Moran | Win | KO | 1 (10) |
| March 2, 1939 | Domenico Ceccarelli | Win | KO | 1 (10) |
| March 16, 1939 | Marty Simmons | Win | UD | 10 |
| April 20, 1939 | Teddy Yarosz | Loss | UD | 10 |
| July 21, 1939 | Jack Coggins | NC | NC | 8 (10) |
| September 1, 1939 | Jack Coggins | Win | PTS | 10 |
| September 22, 1939 | Bobby Seaman | Win | TKO | 7 (10) |
| November 13, 1939 | Freddie Dixon | Draw | TD | 8 (10) |
| November 27, 1939 | Billy Day | Win | KO | 1 (10) |
| December 7, 1939 | Honeyboy Jones | Win | PTS | 10 |
| December 29, 1939 | Shorty Hogue | Loss | PTS | 6 |

| Date | Opponent | Result | Type | Round |
|---|---|---|---|---|
| March 30, 1940 | Jack McNamee | Win | TKO | 4 (12) |
| April 18, 1940 | Ron Richards | Win | TKO | 10 (12) |
| May 9, 1940 | Atilio Sabatino | Win | TKO | 5 (12) |
| May 18, 1940 | Joe Delaney | Win | KO | 2 (12) |
| May 27, 1940 | Frank Lindsay | Win | KO | 4 (12) |
| June 27, 1940 | Fred Henneberry | Win | TKO | 7 (12) |
| July 11, 1940 | Ron Richards | Win | PTS | 12 |
| October 18, 1940 | Pancho Ramirez | Win | TKO | 5 (10) |
| January 17, 1941 | Clay Rowan | Win | KO | 1 (10) |
| January 31, 1941 | Shorty Hogue | Loss | PTS | 10 |
| February 20, 1941 | Eddie Booker | Draw | PTS | 10 |
| January 28, 1942 | Bobby Britt | Win | KO | 3 (10) |
| February 27, 1942 | Al Globe | Win | TKO | 2 (10) |
| March 18, 1942 | Jimmy Casino | Win | TKO | 5 (10) |
| October 30, 1942 | Shorty Hogue | Win | TKO | 2 (10) |
| November 6, 1942 | Tabby Romero | Win | KO | 2 (10) |
| November 27, 1942 | Jack Chase | Win | UD | 10 |
| December 11, 1942 | Eddie Booker | Draw | PTS | 12 |
| May 8, 1943 | Jack Chase | Win | UD | 15 |
| July 22, 1943 | Big Boy Hogue | Win | TKO | 5 (10) |
| July 28, 1943 | Eddie Cerda | Win | KO | 3 (10) |
| August 2, 1943 | Jack Chase | Loss | UD | 15 |
| August 16, 1943 | Aaron Wade | Loss | PTS | 10 |
| November 4, 1943 | Kid Hermosillo | Win | TKO | 5 (10) |
| November 26, 1943 | Jack Chase | Win | MD | 10 |
| January 7, 1944 | Amado Rodriguez | Win | KO | 1 (10) |
| January 21, 1944 | Eddie Booker | Loss | TKO | 8 (10) |
| March 24, 1944 | Roman Starr | Win | TKO | 2 (10) |
| April 21, 1944 | Charley Burley | Loss | PTS | 10 |
| May 19, 1944 | Kenny LaSalle | Win | PTS | 10 |
| August 11, 1944 | Lloyd Kip Mays | Win | KO | 3 (10) |
| August 18, 1944 | Jimmy Hayden | Win | KO | 5 (10) |
| September 1, 1944 | Battling Monroe | Win | KO | 6 (10) |
| December 18, 1944 | Nate Bolden | Win | UD | 10 |
| January 11, 1945 | Joey Jones | Win | TKO | 2 (8) |
| January 29, 1945 | Bob Jacobs | Win | TKO | 9 (10) |
| February 12, 1945 | Napoleon Mitchell | Win | KO | 6 (8) |
| April 2, 1945 | Nate Bolden | Win | UD | 10 |
| April 23, 1945 | Teddy Randolph | Win | TKO | 9 (10) |
| May 21, 1945 | Lloyd Marshall | Win | UD | 10 |
| June 18, 1945 | George Kochan | Win | TKO | 6 (10) |
| June 26, 1945 | Lloyd Marshall | Win | TKO | 10 (10) |
| August 22, 1945 | Jimmy Bivins | Loss | KO | 6 (10) |
| September 17, 1945 | Cocoa Kid | Win | KO | 8 (10) |
| October 22, 1945 | Holman Williams | Loss | MD | 10 |
| November 12, 1945 | O'Dell Riley | Win | KO | 6 (10) |
| November 26, 1945 | Holman Williams | Win | TKO | 11 (12) |
| December 13, 1945 | Colion Chaney | Win | KO | 5 (10) |

| | | | | |
|---|---|---|---|---|
| January 28, 1946 | Curtis Sheppard | Win | UD | 12 |
| February 5, 1946 | George Parks | Win | KO | 1 (10) |
| May 2, 1946 | Vern Escoe | Win | TKO | 7 (10) |
| **Date** | **Opponent** | **Result** | **Type** | **Round** |
| May 20, 1946 | Ezzard Charles | Loss | UD | 10 |
| August 19, 1946 | Buddy Walker | Win | KO | 4 (10) |
| September 9, 1946 | Jimmy O'Brien | Win | TKO | 2 (10) |
| October 23, 1946 | Billy Smith | Draw | PTS | 12 |
| November 6, 1946 | Jack Chase | Draw | PTS | 10 |
| March 18, 1947 | Jack Chase | Win | KO | 9 (10) |
| April 11, 1947 | Rusty Payne | Win | PTS | 10 |
| May 5, 1947 | Ezzard Charles | Loss | MD | 10 |
| June 16, 1947 | Curtis Sheppard | Win | UD | 10 |
| July 14, 1947 | Bert Lytell | Win | UD | 10 |
| July 30, 1947 | Bobby Zander | Win | PTS | 12 |
| September 8, 1947 | Jimmy Bivins | Win | TKO | 8 (10) |
| November 10, 1947 | George Fitch | Win | TKO | 6 (10) |
| January 13, 1948 | Ezzard Charles | Loss | KO | 8 (15) |
| April 12, 1948 | Dusty Wilkerson | Win | TKO | 7 (10) |
| April 19, 1948 | Charley Williams | Win | KO | 7 (10) |
| May 5, 1948 | Billy Smith | Win | UD | 10 |
| June 2, 1948 | Leonard Morrow | Loss | KO | 1 (12) |
| June 28, 1948 | Jimmy Bivins | Win | MD | 10 |
| August 2, 1948 | Ted Lowry | Win | UD | 10 |
| September 20, 1948 | Billy Smith | Win | KO | 4 (10) |
| October 15, 1948 | Henry Hall | Loss | PTS | 10 |
| November 1, 1948 | Lloyd Gibson | Loss | DQ | 4 (10) |
| November 15, 1948 | Henry Hall | Win | UD | 10 |
| December 6, 1948 | Bob Amos | Win | UD | 10 |
| December 27, 1948 | Charley Williams | Win | KO | 7 (10) |
| January 10, 1949 | Alabama Kid | Win | KO | 4 (10) |
| January 31, 1949 | Bob Satterfield | Win | KO | 3 (10) |
| March 4, 1949 | Alabama Kid | Win | KO | 3 (10) |
| March 23, 1949 | Dusty Wilkerson | Win | TKO | 6 (10) |
| April 11, 1949 | Jimmy Bivins | Win | KO | 8 (10) |
| April 26, 1949 | Harold Johnson | Win | UD | 10 |
| June 13, 1949 | Clinton Bacon | Loss | DQ | 6 (10) |
| June 27, 1949 | Bob Sikes | Win | TKO | 3 (10) |
| July 29, 1949 | Esco Greenwood | Win | TKO | 2 (10) |
| October 4, 1949 | Bob Amos | Win | UD | 10 |
| October 24, 1949 | Phil Muscato | Win | KO | 6 (10) |
| December 6, 1949 | Charley Williams | Win | KO | 8 (10) |
| December 13, 1949 | Leonard Morrow | Win | KO | 10 (15) |
| January 31, 1950 | Bert Lytell | Win | UD | 10 |
| July 31, 1950 | Vernon Williams | Win | KO | 2 (10) |
| January 2, 1951 | Billy Smith | Win | TKO | 8 (10) |
| January 28, 1951 | John Thomas | Win | KO | 1 (10) |
| February 21, 1951 | Jimmy Bivins | Win | TKO | 9 (10) |
| March 13, 1951 | Abel Cestac | Win | UD | 10 |

| | | | | |
|---|---|---|---|---|
| April 26, 1951 | Herman Harris | Win | TKO | 4 (10) |
| May 14, 1951 | Art Henri | Win | TKO | 4 (10) |
| June 9, 1951 | Abel Cestac | Win | RTD | 9 (12) |
| June 23, 1951 | Karel Sys | Draw | PTS | 12 |
| July 7, 1951 | Alberto Santiago Lovell | Win | KO | 1 (12) |

| **Date** | **Opponent** | **Result** | **Type** | **Round** |
|---|---|---|---|---|
| July 14, 1951 | Vicente Quiroz | Win | RTD | 6 (10) |
| July 26, 1951 | Victor Carabajal | Win | KO | 3 (12) |
| July 28, 1951 | Americo Capitanelli | Win | KO | 3 (10) |
| August 5, 1951 | Rafael Miranda | Win | TKO | 4 (10) |
| August 17, 1951 | Alfredo Lagay | Win | KO | 3 (10) |
| September 5, 1951 | Embrel Davidson | Win | KO | 1 (10) |
| September 25, 1951 | Harold Johnson | Win | UD | 10 |
| October 29, 1951 | Chubby Wright | Win | TKO | 7 (10) |
| December 10, 1951 | Harold Johnson | Loss | UD | 10 |
| January 29, 1952 | Harold Johnson | Win | UD | 10 |
| February 27, 1952 | Jimmy Slade | Win | UD | 10 |
| May 19, 1952 | Bob Dunlap | Win | KO | 6 (10) |
| June 26, 1952 | Clarence Henry | Win | UD | 10 |
| July 25, 1952 | Clinton Bacon | Win | TKO | 4 (10) |
| December 17, 1952 | Joey Maxim | Win | UD | 15 |
| January 27, 1953 | Toxie Hall | Win | KO | 4 (10) |
| February 16, 1953 | Leonard Dugan | Win | TKO | 8 (10) |
| March 3, 1953 | Sonny Andrews | Win | TKO | 5 (10) |
| March 11, 1953 | Niño Valdés | Win | UD | 10 |
| March 17, 1953 | Al Spaulding | Win | KO | 3 (10) |
| March 30, 1953 | Frank Buford | Win | TKO | 9 (10) |
| June 24, 1953 | Joey Maxim | Win | UD | 15 |
| August 22, 1953 | Rinaldo Ansaloni | Win | TKO | 4 (10) |
| September 12, 1953 | Dogomar Martinez | Win | PTS | 10 |
| January 27, 1954 | Joey Maxim | Win | UD | 15 |
| March 9, 1954 | Bob Baker | Win | TKO | 9 (10) |
| June 7, 1954 | Bert Whitehurst | Win | TKO | 6 (10) |
| August 11, 1954 | Harold Johnson | Win | TKO | 14 (15) |
| May 2, 1955 | Niño Valdés | Win | PTS | 15 |
| June 22, 1955 | Bobo Olson | Win | KO | 3 (15) |
| September 21, 1955 | Rocky Marciano | Loss | KO | 9 (15) |
| February 20, 1956 | Howard King | Win | UD | 10 |
| February 27, 1956 | Bob Dunlap | Win | KO | 1 (10) |
| March 17, 1956 | Frankie Daniels | Win | UD | 10 |
| March 27, 1956 | Howard King | Win | UD | 10 |
| April 10, 1956 | Willie Bean | Win | TKO | 5 (10) |
| April 16, 1956 | George Parmentier | Win | TKO | 3 (10) |
| April 26, 1956 | Sonny Andrews | Win | KO | 4 (10) |
| April 30, 1956 | Gene Thompson | Win | KO | 3 (10) |
| June 5, 1956 | Yolande Pompey | Win | TKO | 10 (15) |
| July 25, 1956 | James J. Parker | Win | TKO | 9 (15) |
| September 8, 1956 | Roy Shire | Win | TKO | 3 (10) |
| November 30, 1956 | Floyd Patterson | Loss | KO | 5 (15) |

| | | | | |
|---|---|---|---|---|
| May 1, 1957 | Hans Kalbfell | Win | UD | 10 |
| June 2, 1957 | Alain Cherville | Win | TKO | 6 (10) |
| September 20, 1957 | Tony Anthony | Win | KO | 7 (15) |
| October 31, 1957 | Ralph Hooker | Win | TKO | 5 (10) |
| November 5, 1957 | Eddie Cotton | Win | UD | 10 |
| November 29, 1957 | Roger Rischer | Win | KO | 4 (10) |
| January 18, 1958 | Luis Ignacio | Win | PTS | 10 |
| **Date** | **Opponent** | **Result** | **Type** | **Round** |
| February 1, 1958 | Julio Neves | Win | KO | 3 (10) |
| March 4, 1958 | Bert Whitehurst | Win | TKO | 10 (10) |
| March 10, 1958 | Bob Albright | Win | TKO | 7 (10) |
| May 2, 1958 | Willi Besmanoff | Win | SD | 10 |
| May 17, 1958 | Howard King | Win | UD | 10 |
| May 26, 1958 | Charley Norkus | Win | UD | 10 |
| June 9, 1958 | Howard King | Win | UD | 10 |
| August 4, 1958 | Howard King | Draw | PTS | 10 |
| December 10, 1958 | Yvon Durelle | Win | KO | 11 (15) |
| March 9, 1959 | Sterling Davis | Win | TKO | 3 (10) |
| August 12, 1959 | Yvon Durelle | Win | KO | 3 (15) |
| May 25, 1960 | Willi Besmanoff | Win | TKO | 10 (15) |
| September 13, 1960 | George Abinet | Win | RTD | 3 (10) |
| October 29, 1960 | Giulio Rinaldi | Loss | PTS | 10 |
| November 28, 1960 | Buddy Turman | Win | UD | 10 |
| March 25, 1961 | Buddy Turman | Win | UD | 10 |
| June 10, 1961 | Giulio Rinaldi | Win | UD | 15 |
| October 23, 1961 | Pete Rademacher | Win | TKO | 6 (10) |
| March 30, 1962 | Alejandro Lavorante | Win | TKO | 10 (10) |
| May 7, 1962 | Howard King | Win | KO | 1 (10) |
| May 28, 1962 | Willie Pastrano | Draw | MD | 10 |
| November 15, 1962 | Muhammad Ali | Loss | TKO | 4 (12) |
| March 15, 1963 | Mike DiBiase | Win | TKO | 3 (10) |

CPSIA information can be obtained
at www.ICGtesting.com
Printed in the USA
LVHW051830170723
752373LV00012B/642

9 781958 425459